Moshi Monsters™

Daily Challenge

365 Puzzles

D0263171

To claim your exclusive virtual gift,
go to the sign-in page of
MOSHIMONSTERS.COM
and enter the surname of the Monster
who wrote the puzzles in this book!
Your surprise free gift will appear
in your treasure chest!

SUNBIRD
PENGUIN

Published by Ladybird Books Ltd 2012
A Penguin Company
Penguin Books Ltd, 80 Strand, London, WC2R 0RL, UK
Penguin Group (USA) Inc., 375 Hudson Street, New York 10014, USA
Penguin Books Australia Ltd, Camberwell Road, Camberwell,
Victoria 3124, Australia (A division of Pearson Australia Group Pty Ltd)
Penguin Group (NZ), 67 Apollo Drive, Rosedale, Auckland 0632,
New Zealand (a division of Pearson New Zealand Ltd)
Canada, India, South Africa

Sunbird is a trademark of Ladybird Books Ltd

Written by Mandy Archer

www.ladybird.com

ISBN: 9781409390947
002
Printed in Great Britain

Greetings Monster Puzzlers!

Tamara Tesla

here, Monstro City's very own **brainiac scientist**, mental mathematician and puzzle plotter!

I've been holed up in my Observatory lab for months, frantically experimenting and computing a year's worth of **EXTREME** puzzles. That's right, dear Monsters, inside this fangtastic book there are 365 quizzes, wordsearches and crosswords to get you scratching your head, wrinkling your forehead and tugging your chins.

As well as Scare Squares and other Moshi classics, this Daily Challenge book is **oozing with new games,** contests and triv tests. I've calculated each new puzzle so that it's tough enough to even get the slickest Super Moshi banging the walls and groaning with frustration! It's a **total brain buzz!** My antennae are sparking with excitement at the very notion . . .

So what are you waiting for? Give your Monster an online workout at the Puzzle Palace, grab a pen or pencil, then get scribbling.

Best of luck!

TAMARA TESLA

Pony Picks

Ponies are pretty, playful and perfect to pet. Saddle up for this game and you'll find out all you need to know about your fave horsey Moshlings! Look at the list of pony words, then tick each one off as you find it in the letter grid.

A	S	E	L	P	P	A	Y	D	N	A	C
C	L	O	U	D	N	I	N	E	Q	U	I
M	G	A	N	G	R	A	N	G	E	L	W
A	D	L	V	E	I	J	O	L	K	I	L
G	A	L	T	E	N	G	D	X	N	F	U
I	N	I	G	R	R	O	I	G	E	G	F
C	N	C	F	B	O	R	S	U	J	B	E
A	D	S	P	N	N	S	O	E	T	U	C
L	O	I	S	M	G	L	E	E	B	H	A
S	A	R	A	I	T	I	E	T	A	A	R
K	M	P	C	X	V	A	N	L	T	R	G
X	H	A	U	G	H	T	Y	G	E	E	L

☐ ANGEL
☐ CANDY APPLES
☐ CLOUD NINE
☐ CUTE
☐ GIGI
☐ GRACEFUL
☐ HAUGHTY
☐ MAGICAL
☐ MR SNOODLE
☐ NOSEBAG
☐ PRISCILLA
☐ ROSETTE
☐ TIARAS
☐ TAILS
☐ WINGS

Wild Word Challenge

How many words of three letters or more can you make out of the sentence below? Give yourself no more than three minutes. If you're a true Moshi maniac, see how many you can come up with in two!

I LUUURVE EXTREME PUZZLES!

REST · SEEM · DIZZ

Fancy a bet?

Raarghly, the owner of the Games Starcade, doesn't reckon any of you can top twelve words.
Game on!

Moshi Jumble

Which trio of cute Moshi Monsters are hiding in the jumbled jigsaw?

1. Katsuma ....

2. ....

3. ....

Got 'em all? Aww shucks, you're good!

Naughty Ninja!

Chop Chop is monkeying around again! Today he's doing his best to trip up as many Moshi Monsters as he can using his favourite weapon – squidgy banana skins. Count up the 'nanas to see how many unsuspecting citizens of Monstro City he's already sent flying. Chop Chop the Cheeky Chimp has dropped …

Banana skins.

Purplexing Puzzle

Prof. Purplex has scrawled nine numbers on his blackboard between 36 and 96 in no particular order. The boffin-brained Moshling wants the digits to increase by five each time.

91

36

71

76

86

56

61

96

46

Work out which four numbers are missing from the board and then write them into the boxes below.

SUPER TOUGH!

Eyes Spy

Roary Scrawl needs eyes in the back of his head to keep up with all the comings and goings in Monstro City. Luckily the Editor-in-Chief at the *Daily Growl* has that and more! Just when he thought that he had too many eyeballs to count, a ton more have turned up. Can you count them all?

Write the total in this box.

Remember:

If you get stuck, ask for help — four eyes are better than one!

Gross-ery Giggles

008

SUPER TOUGH!

That shopkeeper in the Gross-ery Store on Main Street is one slippery customer! Every time he goes to work he ends up spilling the merchandise and making a real mess of things.
Do you know the crazy cashier's name? Use the Rox price tag code to spell it out.

13 2 20 14 14 7 26   11 20 10 10 7 26 13 20 2

Price tag key

A = 27-24	J = 14+7	S = 46-33 .....
B = 9+1	K = 4x3	T = 11x2 .....
C = 16÷4	L = 28÷4	U = 73-58 .....
D = 13+6	M = 13+11	V = 4x4 .....
E = 15+11	N = 64÷32	W = 88÷8 .....
F = 100÷4	O = 2x10	X = 54÷9 .....
G = 3x3	P = 45÷9	Y = 9+8 .....
H = 71-70	Q = 3+5	Z = 7x2 .....
I = 2x9	R = 16+7	

MYSTERY MOSHLING

I live underwater,
I have many spikes.
Bizarrely, old flip-flops,
Are one of my 'likes',
I love blowing raspberries,
Plus I'm quite scatty,
They call me a bubblefish,
And say that I'm batty,
I'm a cute little Moshling,
I make a great pet,
But don't ask my name
I don't know. I forget!

WHO AM I?
THE MYSTERY MOSHLING IS

....

Moshling Memory Game

It's time to check your memory skills. Give yourself sixty seconds to look closely at this scene showing Hansel the Psycho Gingerboy running for his life. Oh crumbs! Now turn over the page and see if you can answer the quiz questions.

Moshling Memory Game cont...

1. How many flowers are in the picture?..................................

2. How many buttons does Hansel have?..................................

3. Which Moshling is leading the chase?..................................

4. What has happened to Hansel's head?..................................

5. How many clouds are in the sky?..................................

6. Which Moshling is last over the hill?..................................

011

Zommer Tongue Twister

Can you repeat this droolly ditty ten times without tripping over your tongue?

The fab Fluffie Flumpy fell for the funny Fishie Fumble!

Odd Oddie Out

A.

E.

Eight odd Oddies, standing in a row, one of them is not the same, so which of these should go?

B.

F.

C.

G.

D.

H.

Draw a circle around the wrong Sweet Ringy Thingy.

SCARE SQUARES

THIS FANGTASTICALLY DEVILISH PUZZLE WILL GET YOUR BRAIN LAVA BUBBLING – GUARANTEED! TAKE A CLOSE LOOK AT THIS SHAPE FRENZY. HOW MANY SQUARES CAN YOU COUNT?

SUPER TOUGH!

Bubble Trouble

Brain still bubbling with enthusiasm? Give it a total fry with this extreme Bubble Trouble puzzle! Study the bubbles, then tackle each of the questions below.

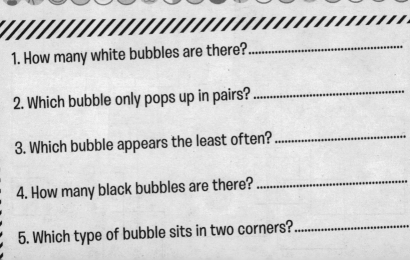

1. How many white bubbles are there? ....

2. Which bubble only pops up in pairs? ....

3. Which bubble appears the least often? ....

4. How many black bubbles are there? ....

5. Which type of bubble sits in two corners? ....

Glumps Crossword

Dr. Strangeglove's naughty minions have bumped and blobbed their way into this perfectly innocent crossword! Root out the devious dozen by reading the clues and filling in the word grid.

Finding it fiendishly tough? Use the anagram clues to help you.

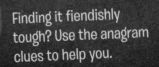

Across

1. Blue glump with bristly facial fuzz. (TICOSHUAM)
2. Snaggle-toothed brute that hates everything. (KOORC)
3. Punch-drunk Glump known for his Scarface Smashes. (RIBEURS)
4. Fearsome ball of dark-hearted fury. (LCKBA AJCK)
5. Badly-behaved blob with a face like squished blueberry. (POBOYL)
6. Raucous reprobate with an icky-sticky tongue. (EGOPD)

Down

1. A-grade student from the School of Drool. (CEFAFKAER)
2. Glump with three eyes, buck teeth and stupid hair. (FIFSUQ)
3. One eyed blob of badness with gloop green lips. (LHIIFSPS)
4. Dimwit with a silly pink quiff. (OBAIF)
5. Vile villain that hides behind a pair of ludicrous goggles. (DEN)
6. The stinkiest Glump in town. (EPAIRT NOPG)

This Poppet has been dancing the night away at a gig by the Moptop Tweenybop Zack Binspin! Afterwards the pretty popster gave the lucky Moshi an exclusive piece of Binspin merch – what was it?

Poppet is so over-excited, she's written about it in code. (Why code? Cos if the rest of Monstro City found out about her new treasured possession, they'd be across town and banging her door down, silly!)

Use this musical decoder to help you work out what Zack gave Poppet.

Write your answer in here.

CADGED A E B BADGE

Fun Park Freakout

OMM! This Furi has got himself lost in the Fun Park and it's almost time for tea! Help the manic Moshi find the right path to the exit so he can get home and start slurping his bowl of Silly Chili.

017

D.

A.

B. C.

Burp!

Fact or Fib?

Superfans grab a pencil and pit your wits against this totally tricky true or false quiz. Are you a Master of Moshi?

1. Oddie is ultra rare.
- ☑ Fact
- ☐ Fib

2. Scamp is a Moshling Puppy.
- ☑ Fact
- ☐ Fib

3. Dewy runs the Yum Yum Kitchen.
- ☐ Fact
- ☑ Fib

4. Buster Bumblechops can't stand Moshlings.
- ☐ Fact
- ☑ Fib

5. The gloved meanie in Monstro City is Dr. Stranglehood.
- ☐ Fact
- ☑ Fib

6. The Super Moshis' secret HQ is in the Volcano.
- ☑ Fact
- ☐ Fib

7. Marshmallow Waterfalls and Grape Gloop Geyser can both be found on Gift Island.
- ☑ Fact
- ☑ Fib

8. Luvlis have stars on the tips of their stems.
- ☑ Fact
- ☐ Fib

BLOCK PARTY

019

This Block Party puzzle is gonna have you running round in squares! Put your finger on the monster in the middle of the grid. Now lead him four blocks east, two blocks north, six blocks west, two more blocks north, one east and then five blocks south. Where does he end up? Draw a circle around the right letter.

			Z		A		
		Y	G	N	W	D	
		T	R	K	M	S	
	B	Q	P	👾	I	J	U
		X	E	L	F	C	
			V	O	U		
			H				

Here Fishie Fishie

This Zommer has set out to bag a soggy new Moshling for his zoo. Which Fishie has the stitch-picking thingamajig got his eye on? Fill in the blanks in the clue questions, complete the letter grid and then read down the shaded column to find out.

Clues

1. Fumble is an acrobatic _ _ _ _ _ _ _.

2. Batty Bubblefish can usually be found swimming in _ _ _ _ _ _ _ _ _ _.

3. All Fishies splash and play in the Potion _ _ _ _ _.

4. Cali loves to munch on seaweed _ _ _ _ _ _ _ _ _ _.

5. Blurp spits out galloons of multi-coloured _ _ _ _ _.

6. Fumble spends his days basking in the _ _ _ _ _ _ _ Lagoon.

7. Cali is a ditzy _ _ _ _ _ _ _ _ _ _ _ _ _.

Line Dance

Take a look at this busy mess of parallel lines, snaking all over the page! Now look again. How many separate lines can you count exactly? Write your answer in the box.

chock-a-block

Horrods sales beauty Mizz Snoots thought she'd have a go at this 3-D cube counting extravaganza, but even her sizeable brain balked at the challenge! Can you count the building blocks stacked up on this page, including the ones hidden beneath others?

SUPER TOUGH!

Write your answer in here.

Crazy Quilt

Tamara Tesla has many hidden talents — aside from being Monstro City's undisputed chemistry queen, she also knows how to quilt! Today the sparky scientist has stitched a design to test your powers of observation to the Moshi MAX. Only one of these quilt squares is unique. Which one?

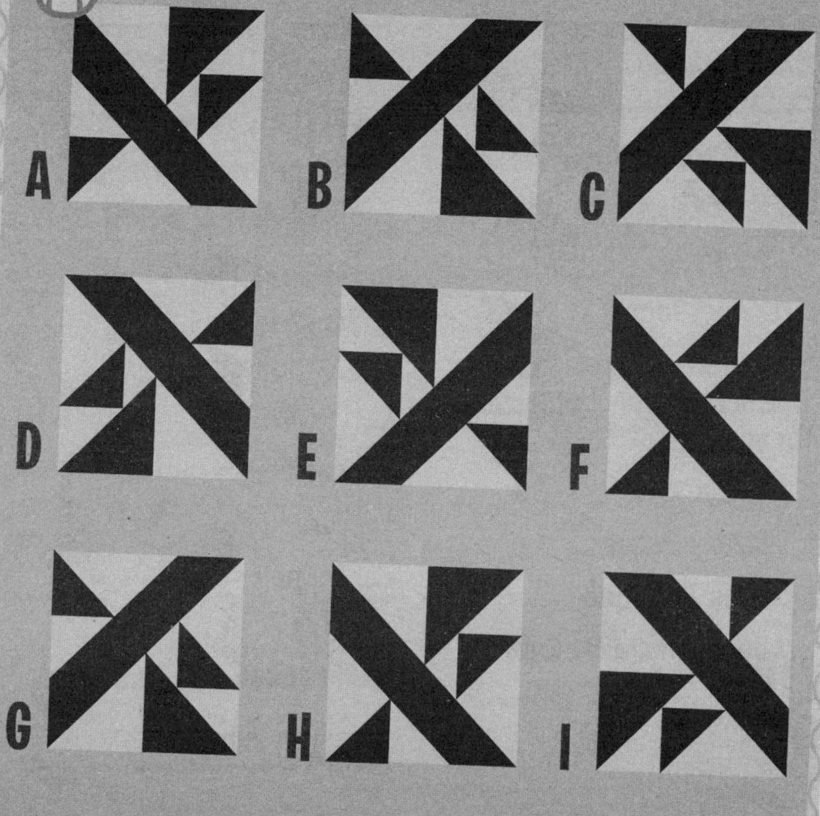

A

B

C

D

E

F

G

H

I

Tricky Trivia

So you think that you're a bona fide Monster clever clogs? Find a stopwatch and see how fast you can get through this Moshi triv test. Start the clock and get ticking!

1. What is the surname of musical sensation Zack?

☐ Binspin

☐ Banana

☐ Attack

☐ Armadillo

2. What is the name of C.L.O.N.C.'s most notorious candy-loving criminal?

☐ Lollipop Lurker

☐ Candy Jaws

☐ Tooth Rot

☐ Sweet Tooth

3. Where would you go to buy Wall Scrawl Alphabet letters for your room?

☐ Yukea

☐ Bizarre Bazaar

☐ Babs' Boutique

☐ Googenheim Art Gallery

4. Who is Roary Scrawl's celebrity girlfriend?

☐ Tyra Finger

☐ Tyra Fangs

☐ Fyra Tangs

☐ Tyra Fang

5. Where can you earn extra Rox on Ooh La Lane?

☐ At the Ice-Scream! store

☐ At the Print Workshop

☐ In the street

☐ At Tyra's Spa

6. Which Moshi wears a mini pair of boots?

☐ Diavlo

☐ Katsuma

☐ Furi

☐ Poppet

Time taken..........................

Score ....

Bushy's Sock Bonanza

Bushy Fandango is packing for another exotic vacation, but before she can rustle up the sock stash she'll need for the sub-zero temperatures, there's a power cut!

Bushy has ten pairs of white socks, ten pairs of black socks, and eleven pairs of blue socks in her drawer, but they're all mixed up and she can't see what's what in the pitch dark.

How many socks does the intrepid explorer need to take before she can be sure to have at least one matching pair?

BREAK THE BLOCKS

Check out this giant block. How many cuts will it take to break the block into twenty-seven individual cubes?

Psst! A single cut can break through multiple blocks.

Vile Vowels

These *Daily Growl* headlines are all missing two crucial vowels. Can you work out what they are? Complete the sentences to discover what's hot off the Monstro City press . . .

The Daily Growl

1. BR_ _ K-IN _T HORRODS:
   DR. STR_NG_GLOV_ SUSP_CT_D!

2. VOLC_NO _RUPTION THR_ _T_NS MONSTRO CITY

3. R_SID_NTS IN UPRO_R OV_R 'PONGY' PIR_T_
   GLUMP N_IGHBOUR

4. MO_ YUKKY R_G_INS GOLD_N MOP TROPHY

5. TYR_ F_NGS _ND RO_RY SCR_WL TO W_D IN
   S_CR_T C_R_MONY?

Moshling Treats

You have a basket containing ten Swirlberry Muffins. You have ten Moshling friends, who would each like a snack. You give each of your pets one Swirlberry Muffin.

After a few minutes each of your Moshlings has one Swirlberry Muffin each, but there is still a muffin remaining in the basket. How is this possible?

Beanie Blob Bargain

You have 969 Rox. How many Beanie Blobs

can you buy at Bab's Boutique? ....

How much money do you have left over? ....

What is your fave Beanie Blob? Red Wolf? Dimple? Caspar?

Write their name in here..

FINE FURNISHINGS

1. YBULFETTR BATNICE

_ _ _ _ _ _ _ _ _ _ _ _ _ _

2. TOFO BLEAT

_ _ _ _ _ _ _ _ _

3. DIEFR GGE GRU

_ _ _ _ _ _ _ _ _ _ _ _

This Katsuma is giving his room a Moshi makeover! Unjumble these words to find out what items he's used to add extra Monstar glamour.

4. AGCIM RRIOMR

_ _ _ _ _ _ _ _ _ _ _

5. ENERG MILES LAPELWARP

_ _ _ _ _ _ _ _ _ _ _ _ _ _ _ _ _ _

6. BARFORUDS RODO

_ _ _ _ _ _ _ _ _ _ _ _

Worldie One Out

This puzzle is totally monu-mental! Read the descriptions below, then decide which of these creatures is not a true Worldie.

1. Most monsters used to think I was extinct, but this ultra-rare, riddle-loving Moshi is alive and well! I love painting strange squiggles on walls and searching for lost treasure.

2. I'm able to play six video games at once, making me pretty hard to beat! If you feed me dehydrated ice cream, I'll DEFINITELY be your best friend!

3. I'm a baby blockhead who lives on Beaster Island. Watch out! Although I try to be helpful, I don't know my own strength. Crr-unch!

4. I chime on the hour every hour. I'm a traditional Moshling with a wonderfully waxed bushy moustache. You might spot me bonging along the banks near Westmonster Abbey.

5. I'm a lip-smackin', ice cream stackin' dreamer with a magical heart-topped crown. I live on Divinity Island, but sow three Love Berries seeds and you might catch me!

cleo

Not a worldie

Rocky

Mini ben

Liberty

Rox 'n' Roll

Can you flip this pyramid on its head? THINK before you doodle - you're only allowed to move three Rox to turn this triangle upside down. Draw arrows to show which ones you would move and where would you put them.

Line Dance

OMM! Wallop's thumping out a beat for another crazy line dance! How many different lines can you count dancing over the page below?

Write your answer in the box.

Sparklepop Brain Burp

Imagine this, Foodie fans:

Coolio is in a band. The first band member is called July, the second is called May. The third band member's name is June. What is the name of the fourth band member?

Coolio

Ade It Up!

Roland Jones buys a new bottle of Wobble Ade every fifteen minutes - that's a whole lotta pop! How many bottles does the crazy monster glug in a week?

Work this one out in your head, puzzlers. Go on, I dare you!

Six Sneaky Snakes

Elder Furi has stepped in to test out your Sneaky Snakes skills! Can you impress the leader of the Super Moshis? Study these six stretchy serpents, then put a star next to the one that is the longest.

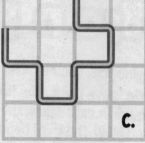

C.

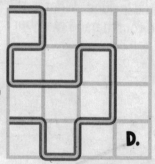

D.

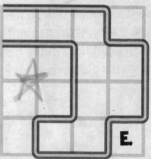

A.

E.

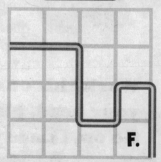

B.

F.

Happy Switchy Day!

This page is a celebration of Switchy Day, a topsy turvy sort of holiday when everything in Monstro City gets twisted back to front!

This year, there were thrills and spills all over town when the shops put on sale a stack of cool Switchy Day merch! Moshis went gaga with excitement.

So what were the hot sellers in-store? Flip the list letters from back-to-front to find out!

1. SNOOLLAB YHCTIWS

SWITCHY BALLOONS

2. REPAPLLAW YMROTS YHCTIWS

SWITCHY STORMY WALLPAPER

3. STRAP ECAF NAMUH

HUMAN FACE PARTS

4. EKAC YRIAF YHCTIWS

SWITCHY FAIRYCAKE

5. GNIWS ERYT

TYRE SWING

6. SREWOLF YELIMS-NU

UN-SMILEY FLOWERS

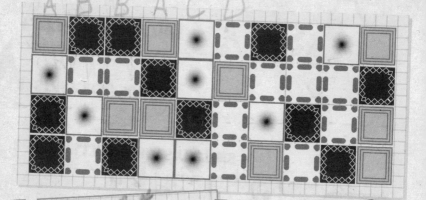

MANIC MATCH

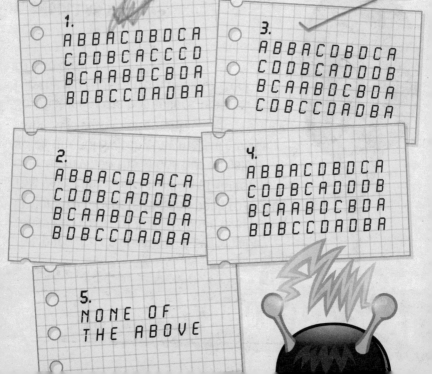

038

Only eagled-eyed Moshis will be sharp enough to tackle this EXTREME pattern puzzle! Study the squares carefully, then see how my computer has represented them in letters below. Which of the printouts represents the pattern correctly?

1.
ABBACDBDCA
CDDBCACCCD
BCAABDCBDA
BDBCCDADBA

3.
ABBACDBDCA
CDDBCADDDB
BCAABDCBDA
CDBCCDADBA

2.
ABBACDBACA
CDDBCADDDB
BCAABDCBDA
BDBCCDADBA

4.
ABBACDBDCA
CDDBCADDDB
BCAABDCBDA
BDBCCDADBA

5.
NONE OF
THE ABOVE

SUPER SCRAMBLE

What monstrous words can you make by rearranging these letters?

A. TASUKAM

KAISUMA
_____

B. FLEDSUGGDUE

_ _ _ _ _ _ _ _ _ _ _

C. RUBLYTFET ILDFE

_ _ _ _ _ _ _ _ _ _ _

D. HGMSOLGOLINOY

_ _ _ _ _ _ _ _ _ _ _ _ _

Game on!

The Moshi Fun Park is worth a visit any day of the year! The Roarkers are always building knockout new games to keep you wriggling and giggling.

This giant wordsearch has been packed full of some of their fave Fun Park thrillers. Can you find them all? The games could be running in any direction — forwards, backwards, diagonally and vertically.

- ☐ **SOLIPSKIER**
- ☐ **BANANA BELLY**
- ☐ **FLASH CAT**
- ☐ **JUMPIT**
- ☐ **KIWITIKI**
- ☐ **PUZZLE SOCCER**
- ☐ **OZEE**
- ☐ **THIN ICE**
- ☐ **WHACK A DOOF**
- ☐ **CAVE CHAOS**
- ☐ **GOLD FISHING**
- ☐ **BLOX**
- ☐ **STAR LINES**
- ☐ **FEED ME**
- ☐ **NEON RIDER**

T	H	I	N	I	C	E	T	G	B	A
V	H	R	G	H	B	G	T	K	A	H
H	J	U	K	S	J	O	D	P	N	X
F	Y	F	H	E	B	L	C	W	A	W
G	Y	K	Y	N	R	D	C	H	N	K
E	N	F	H	I	S	F	S	A	A	Q
R	E	V	B	L	T	I	I	C	B	J
R	O	G	G	R	H	S	O	K	E	O
E	N	J	T	A	C	H	S	A	L	F
C	R	V	G	T	L	I	V	D	L	E
C	I	E	T	S	M	N	K	O	Y	E
O	D	G	I	K	Y	G	I	O	B	D
S	E	E	P	K	G	M	W	F	Q	M
E	R	K	M	V	S	T	I	R	X	E
L	Y	R	U	G	K	P	T	F	E	P
Z	H	F	J	X	M	Y	I	F	E	X
Z	K	P	O	D	P	J	K	L	Z	F
U	T	L	S	G	H	Z	I	O	O	R
P	B	C	A	V	E	C	H	A	O	S

BERT ALERT!

Bert, the shyest worker on Gift Island, has been shovelling presents all day! Can you spot the reserved Roarker before he gets buried in a mountain of gift-wrapped treats?

Moshi Spelling Test

This Furi is a lovable hairball in so many ways, even if he hasn't got the smarts! Check out the Moshi's last spelling test. The monster only managed to get one of these tricky words right. Which one is it?

1. LOLIPOP
2. MONSTEROUS
3. WIERD
4. FIEND
5. GROSE
6. DISSAPEAR
7. HOWEL
8. RYHTHEM

Harumph!

Give Us A ClueKoo!

Only one of these Cluekoos is the obliging little bird that helps our Moshling Gardens grow. Study this flock, then draw a circle around the one that exactly matches the Cluekoo on the scarecrow's sign board.

A.

B.

C.

D.

E.

F.

SCARE SQUARES

ZOMMER HAS PREPARED THIS STITCH-PICKING
SCARE SQUARES BRAINBUSTER ESPECIALLY FOR
YOU. DON'T FREAK! JUST TAKE A LOOK AT THE
JUMBLED SHAPES AND TOT UP THE TOTAL.
EASY PEASY DRIBBLY SQUEEZY!

SUPER TOUGH!

Moshling Zoo

This Moshling Zoo is positively teeming with pampered pets! Study all six of the teeny-weeny critters, then see how many you can name.

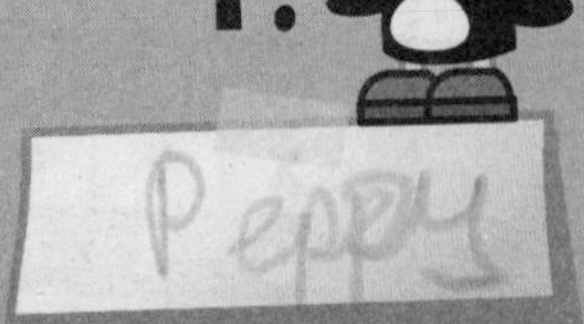

A. Purdey

B.

C. Porkey

D. Honey

E. Plinky

F. Peppy

One of these Moshlings is the odd one out. Can you circle it and decide why it stands out from the crowd?

C.L.O.N.C. CODE

C.L.O.N.C. Monster-enemy number one, Dr. Strangeglove certainly has a lot to answer for! Not only is he a master Moshling Glumper, he's also part of the evil group C.L.O.N.C.!

What do the letters in the wicked organization stand for? Use your powers of deduction to crack the C.L.O.N.C. code!

PIFQFREC CVEAZV

JEKOIV _____

BO REZAWGT PIFGGVIM

__ _____ _____

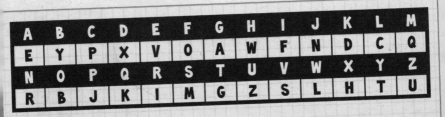

A	B	C	D	E	F	G	H	I	J	K	L	M
E	Y	P	X	V	O	A	W	F	N	D	C	Q
N	O	P	Q	R	S	T	U	V	W	X	Y	Z
R	B	J	K	I	M	G	Z	S	L	H	T	U

A Stroll Down Sludge Street

How much time do you and your monster spend on Sludge Street? There's a whole stack of stores to explore! Pick your fave Moshling and take a stroll into Monstro City, then give this mind-melting quiz a try . . .

1. What store does boom box guy Max Volume hang out in front of?

2. Name two of the arcade games that you can buy in Raarghly's shop.

3. What kind of monster shops at Drop Dead Threads in the Marketplace?

4. Where does Ratty, the purple three-eyed rat hang out?

5. Which posh Sludge Street shop is strictly for members only?

6. Who grazes on the grass next door to the building for rent?

7. Which store does Dewy work at?

8. What wacky wonder smokes in the distance behind Dodgy Dealz?

9. Who is fishing for boots on the jetty at the end of the street?

10. What picture appears on the Marketplace sign?

Doodle Island

Ahoy, me hearties! Cap'n Buck can't stop ya-haaring about his voyage to Doodle Island! According to the ole seadog, it was the most scribbly dibbly place he'd ever explored.

Would you like to create your own picture of the Cap'n's triumphant return in the *Cloudy Cloth Clipper*? Carefully copy each square from the grid to the left into the matching letter square on the opposite page. Keep your wits about ye and even the scurviest landlubber is sure to doodle a ship to be proud of, yarrrrr!

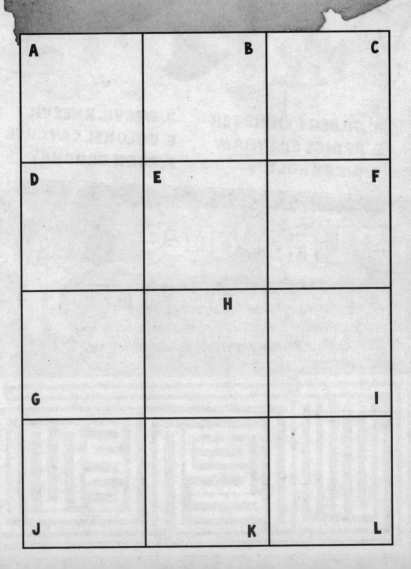

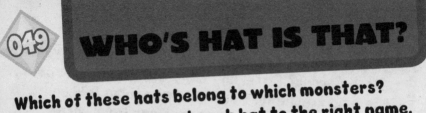

WHO'S HAT IS THAT?

049

Which of these hats belong to which monsters?
Draw a line to connect each hat to the right name.

3.
1.
2.
4.
5.
6.

A. GILBERT FINNSTER
B. PRINCE SILLYHAM
C. DIZZY BOLT

D. WEEVIL KNEEVIL
E. COLONEL CATCHER
F. EGON GROANAY

050 Line Dance

Ping! My lab computer has just devised this
EXTREME circuit of dancing lines to give your a
brain a work-out! Study the grid very closely, then
tot up how many separate lines you can count.

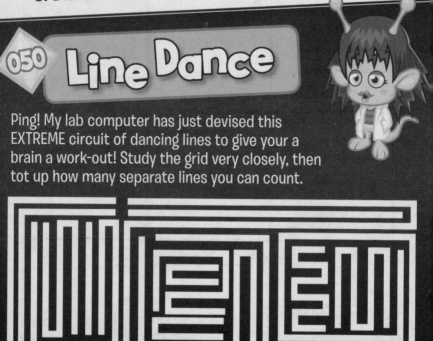

Port Report

The waters around Monstro City are seething with monsters, pirates, mermaids and Fishies. Whether it's down in the depths of Potion Ocean or on the shiny surface of Bubblebath Bay, there's always someone plopping up to say hello!

Put on your snorkel and take a close look at this soggy scene for thirty seconds. Now flip the page, take a deep breath and see if you can fill in The Port report for Cap'n Buck!

Port Report

A-harrr! I looked through my telescope and I did see a fishing boat with three .... fluttering at the stern.

On the water, I spied .... rowing boats, sculling across the water. One of the boats had a .... perched on the brow. There were a pair of wooden .... there too, bobbing up and down on the beautiful briny sea. Made me want to dive in meself! I looked out for Mr Meowford's trawler, but I would wager that he .... out this morning. Suddenly a .... rose out of the shallows and peeped back at me. Could there be a submarine cruising round this port of mine?

I turned my glass to the sky and counted a shoal of .... flying fish. The weather was ....
A good day for seafarin'!

Tricky Trivia

Grab a pencil, set your watch to thirty seconds, then pit your wits against this Puzzle Palace challenge. Can you score top marks with your talent for triv? Game on!

1. Which of these countries does not share a border with France?
☐ SPAIN
☐ ITALY
☐ HOLLAND
☐ GERMANY

2. What is the name of the second Harry Potter book?
☐ PHILOSPHER'S STONE
☐ DEATHLY HALLOWS
☐ HALF-BLOOD PRINCE
☐ CHAMBER OF SECRETS

3. What would you call a baby elephant?
☐ CALF
☐ FOAL
☐ ELECUB
☐ PUP

4. Who was Claude Monet?
☐ A WRITER
☐ A PAINTER
☐ A SCIENTIST
☐ A EXPLORER

5. What's another way of saying two quarters?
☐ TWO-SIXTHS
☐ ONE HALF
☐ ONE THIRD
☐ TWO THIRDS

Noshword Puzzle

Yummy scrummy, it's time for a tummy test! Monsters with rumbling bellies will luuurrrvve this noshi, Moshi crossword. Read each of the clues, lick your lips, then fill in the missing letters.

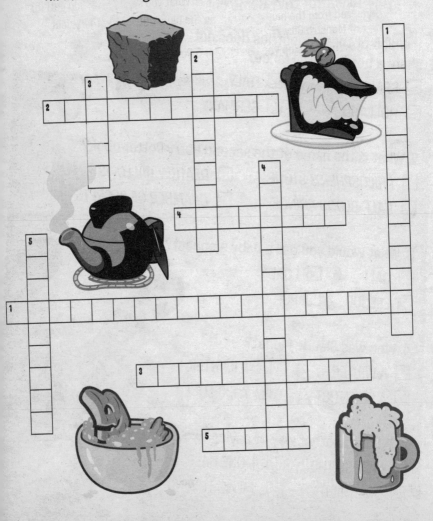

Across

1. A fave Moshi dessert that's full of bite. (9,10)
2. Super sticky with a hint of icky. They might make you sicky. (11)
3. They look wiggly jiggly, but these sweets are as tough as nails. (6, 5)
4. New drink from the makers of Croak-a-cola. (4, 4)
5. We pity the coffee-drinking fool who doesn't sip this! (2,3)

Down

1. A monstrous broth for Hallowe'en. (7,7)
2. Green goo on a stick made by Dastardly Delights. (9)
3. A coloured block of Monster goodness. What you see is what you get! (5)
4. Squeezed from the bluest berries on the bluest bushes in the bluest part of Monstro City. (7,2,4)
5. The best mug of slop you can buy for 5 Rox! (3,1,5)

EYES SPY 054

Stashley Snoozer might be out for the count, but his sharp-eyed hat is always there to cover his back! Right now the natty headgear is trying to count up the eyeballs in this brainbuster while Stashley notches up a few more zzzzzzs.

Can you beat the hat to it?
Count up the eyes, then write the total in this box.

Catch the ↗

That Pixel-Munching Snaffler IGGY has been springing all over the Monstersphere gobbling up pointy arrows left, right and centre! Can you spot where he's been today? Unscramble the jumbled letters to make him spit the cursors out.

▷ HET OPRT

___ _____

▷ FIGT LNDAIS

____ _____ __

▷ HOO AL NAEL

___ __ __ __

▷ NAMI RTEREST

____ _____

▷ LSSDGU TRESTE

_____ _____

▷ ONACVLO

_____ __

Buster Bumblechops' Camera

Our favourite Moshling expert extraordinaire has been on a brand new expedition in search of new specimens to study. He's spotted a clutch of ultra-rare Moshlings through his lens, but can't get close enough to identify them. Can you help him out?

Peer through the camera, then name the Moshlings caught in Bumblechops' lens.

Once Upon A Moshi – Part 1

The Moshi Monsters really are the stuff of fairytales!
Meet Katsuma, Poppet and Diavlo as they star in their
very own activity adventure. Read the first installment of
their story, answering the quiz questions along the way.

Chapter 1
Once upon a time, there were three Moshi
Monsters, aged two, four, and six.
Were their ages even or odd? .... even

Chapter 2
Each little Monster wanted to build a house.
Katsuma wanted to build a house of straw. He went to a shop
and found straw costing four Rox a bundle. He needs nine
bundles.
How much did he spend? .... 36 ROX

Chapter 3

The second little Monster, Poppet, wanted to build a house of sticks. Each bundle of sticks weighed five kilograms. Poppet needed ten bundles.

How much did they weigh? *50k*

Chapter 4

The third little monster, Diavlo, wanted to build a house of bricks. Each wall of his four-sided house needed 100 bricks.

How many bricks did he need?

.... *400*

Chapter 5

Katsuma worked on his straw house for three hours a day for two days.

How long did he work? .... *6 hours*

Gagging for the next installment? Turn to Puzzle 63!

I Should Ken Ken

When you're wheelin' and dealin' at Dodgy Dealz, you've got to have a head for figures! Sly Chance likes to keep his mental arithmetic in tip-top condition by scribbling through Ken Ken puzzles.

Ready to give it a try? It's a bit like Sudoku, but even more EXTREME! This is a 4x4 Ken Ken, so you need to fill the box with numbers from 1 to 4 without repeating numbers in any row or column.

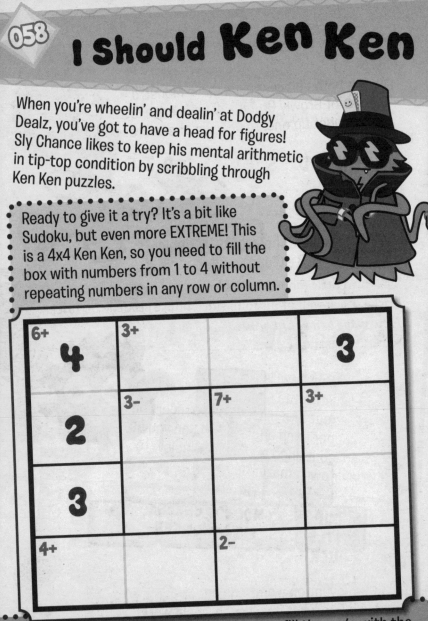

Look at each block or 'cage'. It's your task to fill the cage with the right combination of numbers to reach the 'target number' in the top left corner using the maths instruction shown. Sly has filled in the first cage to get you started, the rest is up to you!

NIFTY SHIFTY

Who's the biggest Monster in Monstro City and the star of Growly Grub Day? Shift each letter of the alphabet up one, to uncover the secret code!

D K L N Q D   S G D   F Q D Z S

_ _ _ _ _ _   _ _ _   _ _ _ _ _

Don't forget to SHIFT before you scribble!
Remember A = B, B = C and so on . . .

D. I. Why?!

Dynamite Moshi Dewi is a DIY fiend - he once constructed a jet-powered jelly bean sorter out of a plastic fork, bangers and mash, a rubber band and a plank! Can you use the letters contained in the items below to create your own amazing invention?

PLASTIC CUP
GLASS BOTTLE
RUBBER DUCK

MOULDY CHEESE
SINK PLUNGER

Give your invention a crazy name, then describe what it will do in Moshi world.

. . . .

. . . .

I Scream, You Scream, We All SCREAM For Ice-Scream!

Giuseppe is working so fast today, he's making ice-screams faster than the Moshis can eat them. How many gloopy gelati can you spot outside his store?

ICE-SCREAM!

Enter your frosty total here.

PEEK·A·POOKY

There are eight Potty Pipsqueaks scuttling around this page, using their eggshell helmets to hide away from low-flying Killer Canaries. Only one of these little Pookys stands out from the crowd. Which one is it?

A.

B.

C.

D.

E.

F.

G.

H.

PRINT WORKSHOP

Once Upon A Moshi – Part II

The Moshi fairytale continues, dear reader...

Chapter 6

Poppet built her house in eight hours. She worked for four days.

How many hours did she work each day? ....

Chapter 7

Diavlo worked for sixteen hours on his house of bricks.

How much longer did he work than Poppet? ....

Chapter 8

Katsuma had his heart set on some spotty floor carpeting. He needed twenty square metres. The carpet cost six Rox per square metre, but there was a sale on at Yukea so he got it for half price!

How much did the carpeting cost in total?

....

Chapter 9

Poppet chose a roll of Switchy Stormy Wallpaper for her room. Each roll could cover sixty square metres, but her room was only thirty square metres.

How much wallpaper did she have left over?

30² = 3/2

....

Chapter 10

Diavlo also got a good deal on his phone bill. It cost him two Rox for the first month, four Rox for the second month and six Rox the third month.

At this rate, what will his bill be for the fifth month? 10 ROX

The Moshi saga continues in Puzzle 70 …

Double-crosser

There's a cheeky Beastie hiding behind this sizzling silhouette! This Moshling is too hot to handle, but can often be spotted soaring through the skies around Mount CharChar on the volcanic island of Emberooze.

C	I	S	K	F	W	O	D	K	Q
M	Q	A	L	H	H	C	G	M	V
H	K	P	B	S	C	Z	F	N	T
F	D	O	Z	S	K	J	Z	L	M
T	J	A	Y	G	A	G	D	J	L
L	U	K	V	K	L	C	X	G	T
Z	V	P	F	J	O	R	L	O	O
A	M	C	P	H	J	G	Z	H	D
V	B	J	T	Y	M	W	C	P	F
H	G	L	V	E	S	G	K	X	Q

Cross out all the letters that appear more than once in this grid. Now rearrange the ones that only appear once to reveal the Moshling's name.

The secret Moshling is

chock-a-block

The construction Roarkers have been building again!
How many blox are in this puzzle?

SUPER TOUGH!

Write your answer in here.

Ickle Limerick

There is a young ninja, a chimp,
Who plays around just like an imp,
This cheeky brown joker,
Will prod with a poker,
Until you scream out like a wimp.

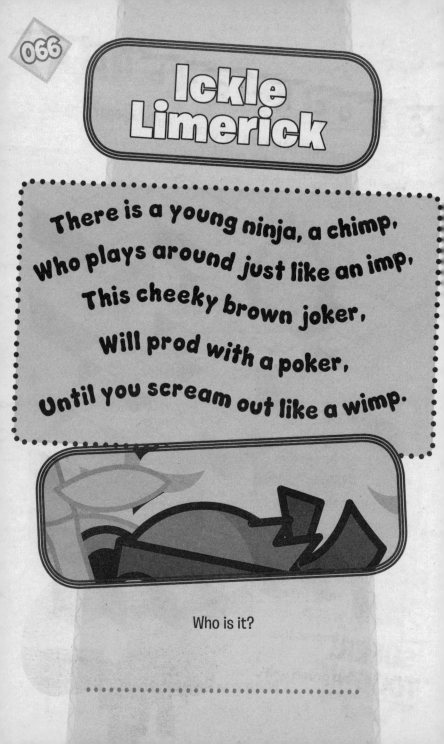

Who is it?

SUPER TOUGH!

Let Sleeping Snufflers Lie

These characters would rather be horizontal than upright.
Try to work out who they are before you drop off too . . .

1.
- He was struck by a sleeping potion as a young sprout.
- His snores help keep bats away.
- He's spent 92% of his life sleeping.
- He looks like a toadstool.

2.
- He likes lullabies.
- His sleepiness is contagious.
- He's spotty and yellow.
- He hangs out with ponies.

3.
- He loves snoozing under the shade of a wacky windmill.
- Forty winks often turns into forty hours.
- He's a Hickopotomus.
- He hates the smell of manure in the morning.

4.
- He appears to be sleeping, but he's really attentive.
- His hat has eyes.
- He has an impressive moustache.
- He wears a green uniform.

SEED SORTING

Gilbert Finnster has an encyclopedic knowledge of Moshling seed codes! Would you like to train your monstrous mind up like the great monster himself? To become a winning Moshi gardener, you need to know your seeds inside out and back to front.

Study this list for thirty seconds:

MOON ORCHID

STAR BLOSSOM

LOVE BERRIES

STAR BLOSSOM

HOT SILLY PEPPERS

DRAGON FRUIT

MAGIC BEANS

DRAGON FRUIT

MOON ORCHID

STAR BLOSSOM

LOVE BERRIES

STAR BLOSSOM

HOT SILLY CHILI

DRAGON FRUIT

MAGIC BEANS

DRAGON FRUIT

Now close the book and see if you can recite all eight types back in the SAME order.

Hansel's Sweet Stash

This rare but rascally Gingerboy can't get enough sweeties! Although he looks cute enough to eat, Hansel is sugar-coated TROUBLE. Check out his stolen stash of liquorice, chocs and candy canes.

How many goodies has he swiped in total?

Once Upon A Moshi – Part III

So the Moshi Monsters have built their houses, but what did the loveable threesome get up to next? The story continues . . .

Chapter 11

When all the work was done the Monsters decided to play a game of 'Jump the Moshi'. The first Monster jumped five metres, the second Monster jumped eight metres, and the third jumped seven metres.

How far did the Monsters jump in total?

___21 m___

Chapter 12

After their busy day, the Monsters were tired. Katsuma went to bed at 9:00 p.m. The others went to bed at midnight.

How much later did Poppet and Diavlo go to bed?

___3 hours___

Chapter 13

The Monsters all woke up ten hours later.

What time did Katsuma get up?

___7:00 am___

Chapter 14

For breakfast the Monsters each munched on six Mice Krispie's. The bag held fifty Mice Krispie's.

How many Mice Krispies did they eat and how many were left in the bag?

18 aten 32 lest

Chapter 15

To work off their enormous breakfast, the Monsters went for a long walk. Katsuma walked three kilometres, Poppet walked four and Diavlo walked five kilometres.

How many kilometres did the Monsters walk in total?

13k

Will the Monsters live happily ever after?
Turn to Puzzle 78 for the thrilling climax!

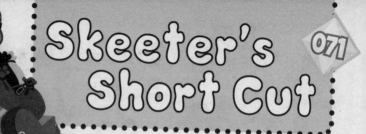

Skeeter's Short Cut

Gift Island's delivery monster Skeeter Rydell is loading his scooter with a stack of presents! He needs to shift the gifts from the factory to the steamer so they can be shipped to Monstro City. Only one of the roads will get him there. Which is it?

A. **B.** **C.** **D.** **E.** **F.**

Gift Island

STICKY STUCKY IN THE MUCKY

Sugary psycho Sweet Tooth is causing madness and mayhem in Monstro City! The serial slurper has poured gooey gum-gum syrup all over Main Street. Which unfortunate Moshlings have got themselves caught in the sticky puddle? Unscramble the letters to find out.

KIIT

MUSKONOS

ILACLIRPS

PRULB

Bubble Trouble

It's extreme bubble time again, puzzle-lovers! This time I've blown a bumper booty to get you fizzing with frustration! Peer closely at the bubbles, then take a pop at the questions below.

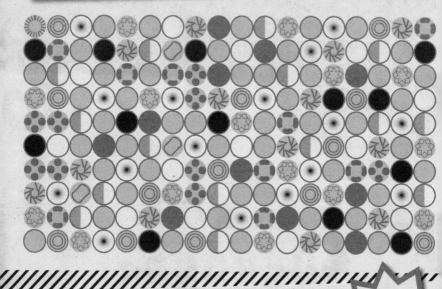

SUPER TOUGH!

1. How many white bubbles are floating along the outside edges? ....

2. What is the rarest bubble? ....

3. How many plain grey bubbles are there? ....

4. There is an even number of only one type of bubble. Which is it? ....

5. Which type of bubble isn't touching a white bubble? ....

Oh 'Eck! It's Ecto

He's elusive and spooky with the ability to materialise anywhere! This friendly Fancy Banshee loves floating around Collywobbles Castle collecting Rox dust.

ECTO ECTO ECTO ECTO ECTO
ECTO ECTO ECTO ECTO ECTO
ECTO ECTO ETO
ECTO ECTO ECTO
ECTO ECTO ECTO ECTO ECTO
ECTO ECTO

Can you work out how many times Ecto has painted his name in the white space above?

075 **Wacky Track**

Put on your colourful legwarmers, crank up the tunes and fill in the missing lyrics to this marvellous melody about the grooviest Moshling around.

DJ ....'s a Disco Duckie,

He'll boogie for you, if you're very ....,

His favourite .... is the Moonwalk,

Don't step on his feet 'cos it makes him ....

WHAT'S IN STORE?

Greetings! The shopkeepers of Monstro City may look unconventional, but they're a very obliging bunch. They like nothing better than welcoming monsters to their humble stores. Whether it's a top-of-the-range Fishy Fountain from Horrods or a bargain Cup O Gruel from the Gross-ery store, they'll go out of their way to give you service with a smile.

Draw a line to match each shopkeeper to their store.

GILBERT FINNSTER

MIZZ SNOOTS

BUSHY FANDANGO

SNOZZLE WOBBLESON

DEWY

MOE YUKKY

YUKEA

GROSS-ERY STORE

PAWS 'N' CLAWS

Horrods

BIZARRE BAZAAR

DIY SHOP

Lucky Numbers

Brain boffin Prof. Purplex wants to see if you're as roarsome with numbers as he is! The wise old Moshling has made up a sequence of digits based on his lucky number, thirteen. Can you put the numbers in the correct order for him?

117   13   26   39   130   52   91   104   143   78   156   65

Once Upon A Moshi – Part IV

It's the final nail-biting installment in the Monsters' puzzle-packed fairytale...

Chapter 16

Katsuma was starting to get crabby. He felt something was wrong. "We're being followed!" he yelled. "Let's run for home!" The Monsters ran and ran, covering four kilometres in eight minutes.

How many kilometres did the Monsters run each minute? _____

Chapter 17

When they got home, Katsuma heard a knock at his door. It was Dr. Strangeglove! "Moshi Monsters, Moshi Monsters, let me come in!" shouted the devious mastermind. "Not by the hair of my chinny, chin chin! replied Katsuma. Now Strangeglove was angry. He huffed and puffed and blew the house down in one minute. Afterwards he marched straight round and blew down the second Moshi Monster's stick house in two minutes.

How many seconds did Dr. Strangeglove blow for in total?

_____

Chapter 18

He might have been bad, but Dr. Strangeglove wasn't stupid. He knew he couldn't blow the brick house down. Instead he thought "I'll just get in my car with the 1963 plates and run this house down!"

If it's now 2012, how old is Strangeglove's car?

Chapter 19

Fortunately for the Moshi Monsters, bricks and mortar won the day – Dr. Strangeglove's car was trashed. The trio decided to use the junked auto to set up a new sideline as scrap metal sellers.

If the car weighs 1420kg, how much money would the brothers make selling scrap metal at 2.72 Rox a kilo? (Round the selling price of scrap metal to the nearest Rox.)

Chapter 20

And so the Moshi Monsters lived happily ever after with their successful scrap-metal business!

If each Moshi earns 1,250 Rox for scrap-metal dealing, how much will they earn altogether?

Word Warp

This Luvli is hoping to notch up her best ever score in this Moshi tick test! Can you help the star-tipped sweetie bag a five out of five? Read each word, then tick the word underneath it that shares the same meaning.

1. What's another word for FLY?

☐ SOAR ☐ DRIVE

☐ SPIDER ☐ SAIL

2. What's another word for SPARKLE?

☐ GLOW ☐ TWINKLE

☐ SHINE ☐ BEAM

3. What's another word for FREAKY?

☐ WEIRD ☐ REGULAR

☐ LOUD ☐ SMILEY

4. What's another word for HAPPY?

☐ CALM ☐ LUCKY

☐ RELAXED ☐ CONTENTED

5. What's another word for MAGIC?

☐ SPOOKINESS ☐ STRANGE

☐ ENCHANTMENT ☐ MAGICIAN

Moshi Mash-Up

Barbecued Bubblefish, this page is over-run with critters! Can you take the first two letters of each animal and put them together with another to make a brand new beastie? There are eight real animal names just waiting to be discovered!

~~PUPPY~~	SEAGULL	ALLIGATOR
HAWK	LLAMA	TURTLE
THRUSH	CRAB	BUFFALO
NAWHARL	WALLABY	OWL
REINDEER	~~MARE~~	
MONKEY	SPIDER	

1 PUMA ....

We've done the first one for you!

2 ....

3 ....

4 ....

5 ....

6 ....

7 ....

8 ....

HAPPY SNAPPIES

Holga has been taking photos all over Monstro City. The Techie can't resist setting up her tripod to snap friends, family — even monsters she doesn't know! Take a look through her latest shots, then answer each of the quiz questions. Cl-iiiick!

1. What type of collection is this?

2. Name this Moshling.

3. Who are these rockers and rollers?

4. These are the doors of which shop?

Tricky Trivia

Find a comfy chair, sharpen your fave pencil, then set your stopwatch to thirty seconds. You've got half a minute to stampede through these triv questions. Think you're a Monstar puzzler? Prove it!

1. When did World War II start?
- ☐ 1945
- ☐ 1914
- ☐ 1942
- ☐ 1939

2. If it's four days before Thursday, what day is it?
- ☐ SUNDAY
- ☐ MONDAY
- ☐ TUESDAY
- ☐ WEDNESDAY

3. What's the capital city of Australia?
- ☐ BRISBANE
- ☐ SYDNEY
- ☐ CANBERRA
- ☐ ADELAIDE

4. What's the world's most widely spoken language?
- ☐ ENGLISH
- ☐ MANDARIN CHINESE
- ☐ DUTCH
- ☐ SPANISH

5. Who invented the telephone?
- ☐ ALBERT EINSTEIN
- ☐ ALEXANDER GRAHAM BELL
- ☐ MARIE CURIE
- ☐ THOMAS EDISON

Time taken.........................

Score ....

Lights Out!

There's been a power failure at the En-Gen power plant, throwing the whole of Monstro City into darkness. While Dizzy Bolt and her Roarkers try to generate more Monstrowatts, it's up to you to shine a light on the Moshis staggering about in the dark. Can you guess who they are?

1. _ _ _ _ _ _ _

2. _ _ _ _ _ _ _

3. _ _ _ _ _ _

4. _ _ _ _ _ _

5. _ _ _ _ _ _ _

6. _ _ _ _

BLOCK PARTY

Ready for another Block Party? Get set, go!

Put your finger on the monster in the middle of the grid. Take the Beastie two blocks north, a block west, five blocks south, two blocks east, one block north, one block east and one block south. Draw a circle around letter marking the monster's destination.

Myth or Mumbo Jumbo?

Ever since he was first inspired by his great uncle, the legendary Moshlingologist Doctor Furbert Snufflepeeps, Buster Bumblechops has been potty about Moshi pets! He's heard every Moshling tale going, some true and some, erm, not-so-true.

Take a read through these claims, then use your Moshi knowledge to decide what's fact and what's fiction.

1. Tiki is colourful, but crafty.
- ☐ True
- ☐ False

2. Rocky does try to be helpful, but Baby Blockheads don't know their own strength.
- ☐ True
- ☐ False

3. General Fuzuki never sleeps.
- ☐ True
- ☐ False

4. McNulty is a master of disguise.
- ☐ True
- ☐ False

5. Doris is obsessed with snaffling pressies from Gift Island.
- ☐ True
- ☐ False

6. Sooki-Yaki is a Slapstick Tortoise.
- ☐ True
- ☐ False

CAN HE NET IT? YES HE CAN!

Colonel Catcher is OTT obsessed with flutterbies! The retired adventurer is always trying to find new species to add to his ever-growing collection. Look at the results of his latest expedition.

How many flutterbies has the Colonel caught in his net?

Psst! Which Moshling has the Colonel trapped by accident?

Puzzling Poem

What kind of Monster do you own? Solve this riddle
to find out if your fave is hiding on this page.

> I've long stripy ears and lightning-fast paws,
> Two rabbity teeth in my rabbity jaws,
> I look pretty cute, but own me and see,
> That my choptastic moves are as cool as can be!

•••

Waldo's Wacky Word Box

089

Whoever heard of a
crossword where the answer
to each clue is filled in across
and downwards at the same
time? Waldo the Tabby
Nerdicat has taken a break
from his algebra to come up
with three teasers for you.

CLUES

1. Zig _ _ _
2. The number of years you've been alive.
3. _ _ _ up! (Something you might say to get
   a Pony Moshling moving.)

Remember to write each answer across as well as down!

Seed Sudoku

Psst! Wanna catch a Moshling? This giant sudoku grid is made for green-fingered monsters!

	LOVE BERRIES			HOT SILLY CHILI
MOON ORCHID	SNAP APPLE	CRAZY DAISY	LOVE BERRIES	MAGIC BEANS
STAR BLOSSOM				CRAZY DAISY
LOVE BERRIES				
	(Scarecrow)		CRAZY DAISY	DRAGON FRUIT
	MAGIC BEANS	SNAP APPLE	MOON ORCHID	STAR BLOSSOM
MAGIC BEANS	MOON ORCHID		(Scarecrow)	SNAP APPLE
(Scarecrow)	CRAZY DAISY		STAR BLOSSOM	MOON ORCHID
	STAR BLOSSOM		MAGIC BEANS	LOVE BERRIES

All you gotta do is make sure that each vertical and horizontal line features a scarecrow and one each of the eight seed types. Happy gardening!

SUPER TOUGH!

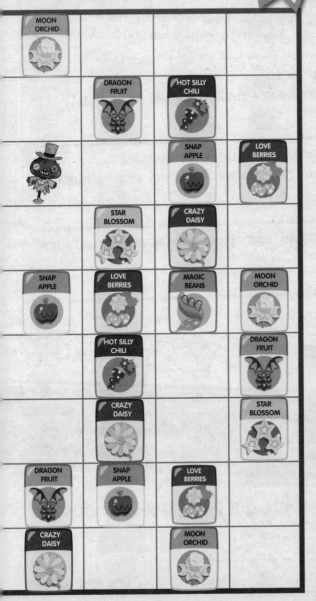

Snoop Scoop!

Wing, Fang, Screech and Sonar spend their nights eavesdropping, reporting all the goriest goss back to Roary Scrawl at the *Daily Growl*. Can you decipher their batty chit chat? It's upside down and back to front!

1. wǝıɓɥʇ uı dǝsʇɹʎ¡
Tuppy Huggishi Durup ǝɐʇs ɥǝɹ oʍu qopʎ

....

2. ʇı's ɐ ɯosɥɯɐɔuǝ ɯɐpǝ uı ɥɐɐʌǝuı
˙ʎpɯɹnℲ puɐ ʎssıʞ dn sʞooH ılɐϽ ıʍoʍ 'ǝʞıꓶ

....

3. ıɥʇuoɯ sıɥʇ ɯıʇɔıʌ ɥʇɹıp Ɯosɥlıuꓵ ǝɓɓıpɓ sǝʇıq ǝɓɓıp⅁

....

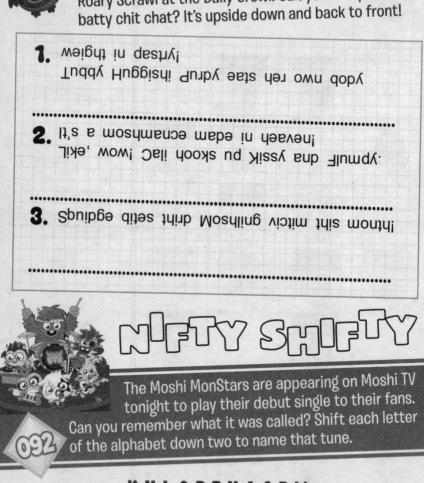

NIFTY SHIFTY

The Moshi MonStars are appearing on Moshi TV tonight to play their debut single to their fans. Can you remember what it was called? Shift each letter of the alphabet down two to name that tune.

K M L Q R P M A G R W

_ _ _ _ _ _ _ _ _ _ _

Don't forget to SHIFT so that A = Y, B = Z and so on...

JEEPERS CREEPERS

Oh no! Jeepers has strayed out of the Barmy Swami Jungle. The Snuggly Tiger Cub needs to find his way back in before anyone spots him. Choose the right path into the jungle so he can get back to sharpening his claws and painting on his stripes.

START

FINISH

Crazy Quilt

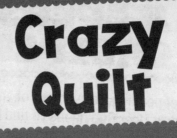

Sorry puzzlers, I just can't stop quilting! Only one of these stitched squares doesn't match the rest - can you pick out the original design?

A

B

C

D

E

F

G

H

I

Shape Shake

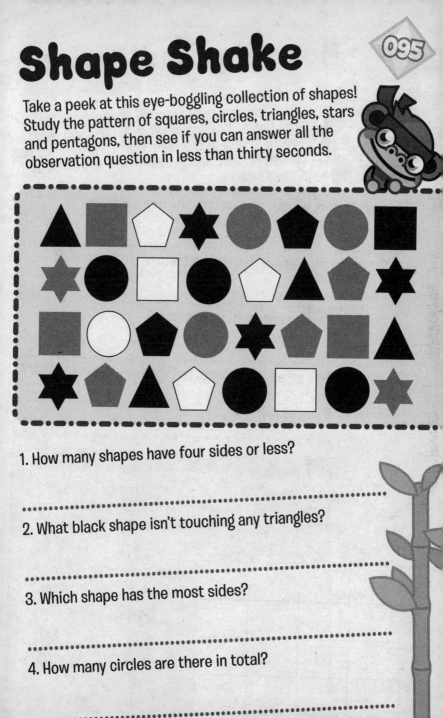

Take a peek at this eye-boggling collection of shapes! Study the pattern of squares, circles, triangles, stars and pentagons, then see if you can answer all the observation question in less than thirty seconds.

1. How many shapes have four sides or less?

....

2. What black shape isn't touching any triangles?

....

3. Which shape has the most sides?

....

4. How many circles are there in total?

....

Moshling Meditations

Prof. Purplex gets through so many books, the Owl of Wiseness has been banned from every library in the land. Now the Moshling has spent hours musing over a new set of birdy brainteasers.

1. What gets wetter and wetter the more it dries?

....

2. What jumps when it walks and sits when it stands?

....

3. What can you catch, but not throw?

....

4. What lives when given food, but dies when given water?

....

ANACROSSAGRAM

What's an anacrossagram you ask? It's an insane back-to-front take on the crossword. Crack the quiz by jumbling up the word clues and fitting the letters into the right place on the grid.

1	2	3	4
2			
3			
4			

Across
1. NOSE
2. FOUR
3. SORT
4. PATE

Down
1. SAFE
2. ROTE
3. SOUP
4. TORN

Fluffy stuff

Aaaaaaaah, Fluffies! These adorable softies are even cute enough to melt Dr. Strangeglove's heart*. Each little snugglepop has got their own itty-bitty ways and itty-bitty habits. How well do you know your Fluffy stuff?

1. Dipsy is a . . .

- ☐ A. Funny Bunny
- ☐ B. Dinky Dreamcloud
- ☐ C. Pluff

2. Pluffs originally come from . . .

- ☐ A. Cotton Clump Plantation
- ☐ B. Cyberspace
- ☐ C. Stinky Hollow

3. Although they look cute, some Fluffies . . .

- ☐ A. could lick you to death
- ☐ B. can bite
- ☐ C. would steal your last Scummi Bear

4. IGGY's favourite snacks are . . .

- ☐ A. pointy arrows
- ☐ B. clumps of wild candiflop
- ☐ C. garlic marshmallows

5. Honey's little frock is covered in . . .

- ☐ A. yellow stars
- ☐ B. green polka dots
- ☐ C. red polka dots

6. The rarest Fluffy is . . .

- ☐ A. I.G.G.Y.
- ☐ B. Flumpy
- ☐ C. Dipsy

7. The most chillaxed Fluffies are . . .

- ☐ A. Funny Bunnies
- ☐ B. Pixel-Munching Snafflers
- ☐ C. Pluffs

8. If they get angry, Dipsy Dreamclouds could . . .

- ☐ A. cast a shadow over your head
- ☐ B. sulk for over two weeks
- ☐ C. rain on you

*or not.

Jurassic Larks

Step back to a time when prehistoric Moshlings roamed the land - hatching eggs, baring their fangs and dodging falling asteroids! This giant wordsearch is riddled with dinotastic words. Peer deep into its recesses, the letters you seek could be running in any direction.

- [ ] SNOOKUMS
- [ ] PREHISTORIC
- [ ] DOYATHINKYSAURUS
- [ ] FOSSIL
- [ ] PLOTAMUS
- [ ] GURGLE
- [ ] DORIS
- [ ] TUMTEEDUM
- [ ] PIPSQUEAK
- [ ] CHOCOLATE MICE
- [ ] ASTEROID
- [ ] POOKY
- [ ] FLUFFLE
- [ ] TOOTH
- [ ] FLAPPASAURUS

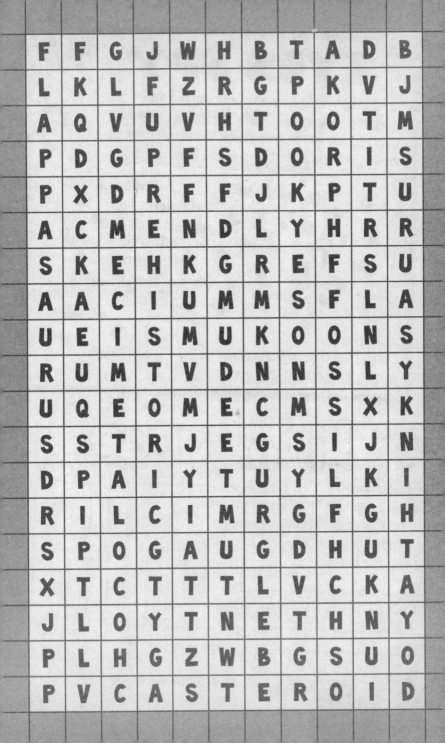

EYES SPY

Could that be Shrewman peeping out from this new count-up quiz? The berry-loving critter only popped out of his tree trunk to search for a quick snack, but look what he's found instead!

Count up the eyeballs, then write the total in this box.

Line Dance

Someone's been scribbling a whole lotta lines on this page! Study the parallel lines until you get cross-eyed.

How many separate ones can you pick out?

A Week Of Wild Words

Ruby Scribblez is not only *Shrillboard Magazine's* smartest roving reporter, she's an author and talk show host to boot!

She is always on the look out for sparkling new vocabulary to pop into her pieces. Help Ruby connect her impressive word list with the right meanings. (And yes, they are all 100% for real!)

1. Brouhaha

2. Somniloquy

3. Whippersnapper

4. Portmanteau

5. Troglodyte

6. Susurrus

7. Floccinaucinihilipilification

A. A small or presumptuous person

B. To describe something as unimportant

C. Cave dweller

D. Suitcase

F. Rumpus, uproar

E. A whisper

G. Talking in your sleep

SUPER TOUGH!

Rhyme Time

There's another Monster hiding behind this potty poem!
Read the verse, then guess which one it could be.

Slouchy and grouchy, a hairball am I,
With a frown on my brow and a tear in my eye
But look deeper still and I'm sure you will see,
That there's no softer monster around than me!

Shuffle Kerfuffle

Her royal sumptuousness Kate Giggleton has got
the perfect day planned! She's getting her nails
done at Tyra's spa, then she's off to Monstro
City's most cultural establishment. Unshuffle
the letters to find out where she is going.

M	I	N	O	E	O	G	G	H	E

PAPPED!

The Underground Disco is thumping tonight! Bubba the bouncer is having to use both of his humungous arms to hold back the budding peppy-razzi. Take a look at these snatched snaps of Bobbi Singsong. Now circle five differences between them.

MOE'S MINUTE MAKEOVER

Congratulations! You've won a Yukea sixty second trolley dash! Moe Yukky has agreed to pay for everything you grab as you hurtle round his homeware store.

Tot up this gift receipt. How much did you win?

```
MANDALA BEIGE WALLPAPER.. 24
GREEN WALL HANGING....... 83
CAMP LAMP................ 110
ARM CHAIR................ 78
FRIED EGG RUG............ 82
CHECKER FLOOR............ 41

TOTAL
ROX.....................
```

Jigsaw Jam

This jigsaw puzzle is driving Furi hopping mad! Throw a rope to the harassed hairball by picking out the shape that will fit snugly into the hole at the top.

A B C D E F

Walk the Plank

SUPER TOUGH!

A-har me intrepid Moshis, Cap'n Buck needs a hand and no mistake! The bridge to the *Cloudy Cloth Clipper* has broken. Can you get everythin' shipshape again? Find a pencil then study the numbers on each plank. Work out the pattern, then write in the missing digits.

3
9
5
20
16
....?
76
456
....?

Got it right? Give yerself a slap on the back!

Growl On The Prowl

He's the name behind some of the most monstrous acts in pop and the toughest judge on the telly - yep, Simon Growl certainly has a lot to answer for! Growl has used his megaRox to build himself the smartest posing pad in Monstro City. Take a tour round Growl Mansion, then crack these quiz questions.

1. How many Monsters and Moshlings are knocking on Simon's door?

....

2. Besides chimneys, what else is sticking out of the roof of Growl Mansion?

....

3. What kind of cereal is in the picture?

....

4. What shape are each of the glass panels on the side of the mansion building?

....

5. How many windows can you see on this side of the house?

....

6.Where is the superstar hiding?

....

Into the Gloop

Greetings, fellow Moshling Hunters!

Four wayward specimens have fallen into the swampy shallows of Lake Neon Soup, but do not fear! Luckily Buster Bumblechops is on hand to fish them out with his net. Look at the shadows in the gloop, then write the correct Moshling name with each shape.

1._____ _____

2._____

3._____

4._____ _____

Waldo's Wacky Word Box

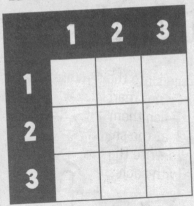

Like a mini crossword but much more fun, here's another of Waldo's wacky word boxes. The answer to each clue is filled in across and down the grid - geddit?

CLUES

1. Female sheep.
2. What Puppies do with their tails.
3. A scrambled, poached or fried treat.

Rox Drop

Gee whiz! He might be a scientific genius, but Dr. Strangeglove sure can be a butterfingers sometimes. The vile villain has dropped his stash of stolen Rox all over the page.

How much has he lost? Count up the Rox, then write the total in here.

Sky Scramble

Which three flying Moshlings are gliding through the skies above Monstro City? Unscramble the potty picture, then write their names in here?

1. ....

2. ....

3. ....

SUPER TOUGH!

Thinky Plinky

One Squeezy Tinklehuff was waltzing along, squeezing a song, when seven more trotted up to join him! Can you spot the first keyboard tickler? He's the only one that is slightly different from the rest.

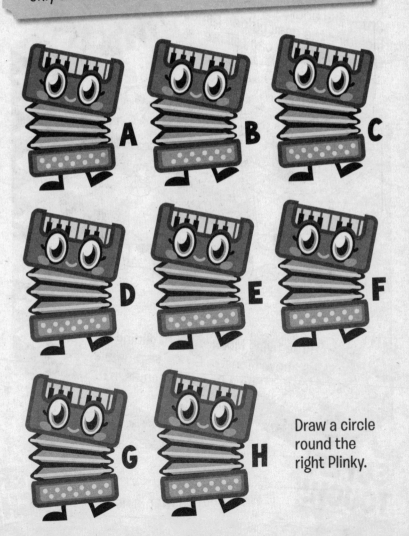

Draw a circle round the right Plinky.

SCARE SQUARES

KATSUMA HAS CHOPPED AND BLOCKED OUT THIS
SCARE SQUARES COUNTING CONUNDRUM. TAKE
TIME TO COUNT UP ALL THE SQUARES THAT YOU
CAN FIND. DON'T FORGET TO INCLUDE THE NEW
BOXES THAT APPEAR IN THE OVERLAPPING LINES.
RRRRR!

SUPER
TOUGH!

Ken Ken Again

Super slick wheeler-dealer Sly Chance has upped the stakes in this Ken Ken quiz. Once you've cracked the rules on Puzzle 58, you'll be ready to try your luck here. REMEMBER – you need to follow the maths instruction to complete each cage, but you can only use the numbers 1 to 4 once in each row or column.

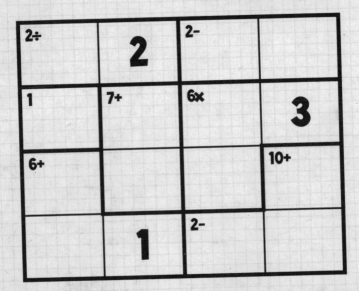

2÷	**2**	2−	
1	7+	6×	**3**
6+			10+
	1	2−	

Go on, take a chance!

MANIC MATCH

118

Manic Matches are made to mash your mind! Study the pattern of squares carefully, then see how my computer has represented their layout in code below. Can you identify the correct print-out?

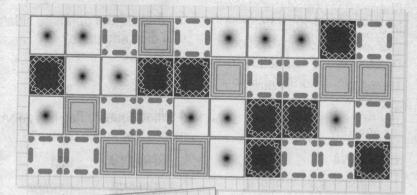

1.
```
DABCBAAADB
DAADDCBBCC
ACBBAADDAB
BBCCCADBBD
```

3.
```
AACCBDDDDB
DAADDCBBCC
ACBBACDDAB
BBCCCADBBD
```

2.
```
AABCBAAADB
DAADDCBBCC
ACBBACDDAB
BBCCCADBBD
```

4.
```
AABCBAAADB
DAABBCBBCD
ACBBACDDAB
BBCCCADBBD
```

5.
```
NONE OF
THE ABOVE
```

Tricky Trivia

It's you versus the clock in this quick triv challenge. To get five out of five, you'll need to be speedier than Weevil Kneevil with rocket jets! Your thirty seconds start . . . now!

1. What is the word to describe a group of lions?

☐ FLOCK   ☐ HERD
☐ PACK   ☐ PRIDE

2. What's the capital of Austria?

☐ VIENNA   ☐ SALZBURG
☐ INNSBRUCK   ☐ BERLIN

3. What do the opposite sides of a dice add up to?

☐ TEN   ☐ TWELVE
☐ SIX   ☐ SEVEN

4. What country flag has got a maple leaf in the centre?

☐ BERMUDA   ☐ USA
☐ HOLLAND   ☐ CANADA

EYE EYE!

The residents of Monstro City are BIG on eyewear! Stroll round town and you'll see some showy specs, glamorous goggles and playful patches on display. Draw a line to match each set of blinkers to the right owner.

1.
2.
3.
4.
5.
6.

A. CAPTAIN BUCK
B. DJ QUACK
C. AGONY ANT
D. SLY CHANCE
E. GILBERT FINNSTER
F. MYRTLE

Potty Prediction

Agony Ant has stared into her crystal ball and chanced upon a prediction that's especially for you! There's no need to grace her palm with Rox – these precious pearls of wisdom need to be earnt …

Use your puzzle powers to make Agony Ant's secret message mystically appear. Some of the letters in the alphabet code have been given to you, the rest you'll need to work out for yourself.

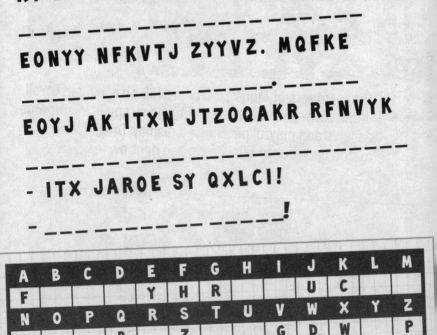

RT ET EOY ZYYV LFNE FKV SXI

__ __ ___ ____ ____ ___ ___

EONYY NFKVTJ ZYYVZ. MQFKE

_____ _____ ____. _____

EOYJ AK ITXN JTZOQAKR RFNVYK

____ __ ____ _____ _____

- ITX JAROE SY QXLCI!

- ___ _____ __ _____!

A	B	C	D	E	F	G	H	I	J	K	L	M
F			Y	H	R			U	C			

N	O	P	Q	R	S	T	U	V	W	X	Y	Z
		B		Z			G	D	W		Y	P

Main Street Mayhem

Time to mosey down Main Street, slap-bang in the centre of Monstro City. Whether you wanna go shopping, try flutterby-hunting or just share a joke with your favourite Roarkers, this is the place to come!

Think you already know Main Street like the back of your hand? Give this brain-burning quiz a bash.

1. Who is having a picnic on the grass?

....

2. What is happening on the plot next to the *Daily Growl* offices?

....

3. Who is waiting to play at the front of Flutterby Field?

....

4. What does the billboard show at the end of the street?

....

5. What are the Moshling seeds being sold from?

....

6. Who sits outside Yukea flicking through the daily papers?

....

7. What building can you see in the distance behind Main Street?

....

Celebration Crossword

Monsters like to party . . . a lot! No matter what the month, there's always something to celebrate in Monstro City. Try and crack all the holidays hidden in the crossword grid, then write them into your Moshi calendar.

Across

1. The day to stamp your foot and jabber like Cap'n Buck. (4,4,1,6,3)
2. A time to celebrate getting crazily confused. (6,3)
3. The only way to start off April. (5,12)
4. A day to revel in the gorgeous green stuff. (5,7,3)
5. The most exciting day of the Monstro year! (8)

Down

1. A time for resolutions and monster madness. (3,5,3)
2. A day when lurve is in the air. (10,3)
3. A fangtastic night to dress up like Fronkenshteen. (9)
4. The ultimate homage to coloured candy. (5,4,3)
5. An annual thank you for rainbows. (3,1,3,3)

---

124 Alphabet Soup

Grab a pen, then see if you can rattle through this loony letter quiz in less than half a minute. Timer starts . . . now!

1. Which vowel is missing from this alphabet?

A ☐   E ☐

O ☐   U ☐

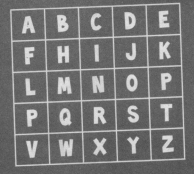

A	B	C	D	E
F	H	I	J	K
L	M	N	O	P
P	Q	R	S	T
V	W	X	Y	Z

2. Which letter appears twice?

Y ☐   P ☐

Q ☐   T ☐

3. Which consonant is missing?

G ☐   L ☐

V ☐   U ☐

Write your time in here ☐

Sweet Spot

Aah, the Candy Cane Caves, where the Sour Cherry River flows and the Candy Floss Grass grows! Now that Sweet Tooth is banished from its scrummy shores, Monsters can visit and make teeny tiny cupcakes to their heart's content.

Take a peek into its sugary shadows, then try and spot six sweet things . . .

1. Purdy licking a lolly. ☐
2. Five Candy Canes. ☐
3. Waldo wading in a wobble-ade stream. ☐
4. Burnie blowing ice scream. ☐
5. An excited Monster edged into an elevator. ☐
6. Cutie Pie creeping into Cupcake Cavern. ☐

Blabbering Birdies

This page is packed with four flapping Birdies and one Moshling imposter. Read the descriptions, name the critters, then find the odd-one-out. Are you feelin' feathery?

Monsters call me a thieving flapper, but I just like to borrow things (a lot!). My golden beak is brilliant at storing stash while my colourful wings make me a tricky Moshling to catch!

Although I look meeker than a melted marshmallow, underneath this helmet is a thrill-seeker with a taste for danger! Feed me a pilchard popsicle, then watch my stunts - I'm wheelie good fun!

I'm a cute little quacker that was born to boogie! Every evening I slick back my feathers with orange sauce, then head out to strut my stuff at the Underground Disco.

Cynical monsters say that I'm just the stuff of legends, but I have been spotted soaring through the pink clouds above Mount Silimanjaro. I'm a pink piece of perfection with white wings and tail.

This little Moshling is brainier than a big brain pie with extra brain sprinkles! I'm happiest rockin' and readin' in an old oak chair or meditating on my wiseness in the trees of Wobbly Woods.

ALL THE OOZE THAT'S FIT TO PRINT!

Roary Scrawl prides himself on the *Daily Growl*s m-o-n-s-t-r-o-u-s reputation! Once the hungry newshound has dug up a sensational story, he checks his sources to make sure that every line is fun, factual and fit to print!

Read these hot headlines. Can you separate the gossip from the good stuff? Tick the stories that sound kosher, then check your answers at the back of the book.

1. DR. STRANGEGLOVE GIVES GENEROUSLY TO SAVE THE GAIL CHARITY

Ooze that's news ☐

Tosh and tittle-tattle ☐

2. BJORN SQUISH TAKES EIGHT-HOUR LUNCH BREAK!

Ooze that's news ☐

Tosh and tittle-tattle ☐

3. CLUEKOO SPOTS ULTRA-RARE MOSHLING VISITORS

Ooze that's news ☐

Tosh and tittle-tattle ☐

4. MOSHI MONSTARS SCORE SMASH WITH 'WELCOME TO JOLLYWOOD'

Ooze that's news ☐

Tosh and tittle-tattle ☐

5. OOH LA LA! KATE GIGGLETON MARRIES PRINCE SILLYHAM!

Ooze that's news ☐

Tosh and tittle-tattle ☐

6. SHY SHREWMAN HELPS SUPER MOSHIS!

Ooze that's news ☐

Tosh and tittle-tattle ☐

Six Sneaky Snakes

Moshi lake legend Tiddles has wriggled his way into this Sneaky Snakes puzzle! Each one of these slippery snakes is a different length. Draw a circle around the longest one.

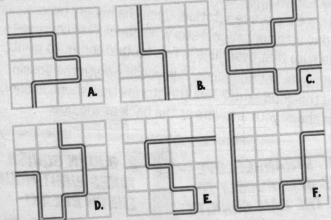

A. B. C. D. E. F.

Hum Plum Fun

Hum Plum works day and night, gathering invisible syrup for her huge brood of kids. When the weeny ones aren't munching on see-through goo, the selfless ladybird keeps them amused with these tortuous tongue twisters.

- Diavlo does daring dares in Dewy's dusty DIY shop.

- Bab's Boutique is bursting with brilliantly buttoned Beany Blobs.

- The coolest Katsumas crave kit from Katsuma Klothes.

Add your own Moshi tongue twister here:

....

....

Boom Boom, Shake The Room!

Ever wondered who that guy is on Sludge Street, rockin' to the beat outside Dewy's DIY Shop? The bodypopper has a mega-amped boom box on his shoulder, shiny trainers and a cap worn in just the right direction to be totally koo-el!

Solve the clues and fill up this letter grid. Read down the shaded column to reveal the stranger's name.

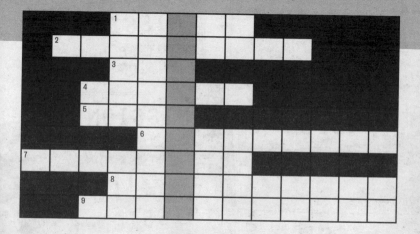

The monster with the moves is _ _ _ _   _ _ _ _ _ _ _ _ _ .

Clues

1 Raarghly runs the _____ Starcade.

2 The fanciest street in Monstro City.

3 Monster money.

4 Lava-topped monster with a fiery temper.

5 Giant, purple-licious sea creature that bobs in a cove near the Port.

6 Colonel Catcher's favourite critter.

7 Trusting Baby Tumteedum.

8 Buster's blustery surname.

9 Heart-shaped seeds that Jeepers can't resist.

MISSIONS MATCH·UP

Super Moshi HQ has been super busy recently, with brand new missions popping up left, right and centre! How many have you assisted on during your time in Monstro City? It's a great honour to be called to help the fight for truth, justice and the right to eat gloop for breakfast.

MISSION 1
MISSING MOSHLING EGG

MISSION 2
VOYAGE UNDER POTION OCEAN

MISSION 3
STRANGEGLOVE FROM ABOVE

MISSION 4
CANDY CATASTROPHE

MISSION 5
POP GOES THE GOO GOO

MISSION 6
SUPER MOSHIVERSITY CHALLENGE

MISSION 7
20,000 LEAGUES UNDER THE FUR

MISSION 8
SPOOKTACULAR SPECTACULAR

MISSION 9
SNOW WAY OUT

MISSION 10
SUPER WEAPON SHOWDOWN

Test out your Super Moshi knowledge by matching up the mission names to the right summaries.

A. Lady Goo Goo has lost her voice! The Super Moshis must investigate.

B. Something precious has been stolen from the Incubation Station! The egg-citing trail leads the heroes into Wobbly Woods.

C. C.L.O.N.C.'s Super Weapon is ready to launch! Is this the end of Monstro City?

D. Strangeglove's airship gets put to bad use when he starts sucking Fluffies out of the skies.

E. It's Halloween and Simon Growl is throwing the party of the year - a spookfest of monster proportions!

F. When Fishies start getting swiped from the beach, Captain Buck gets involved!

G. There's trouble in the Super Moshi Academy when Monstar students start not doing as they are told.

H. C.L.O.N.C. are building a Super Weapon on Mt. Sillimanjaro - can the Super Moshis stop them?

I. Elder Furi disappears, creating cause for concern amongst the Super Moshis!

J. The citizens of Monstro City are getting sick on Dastardly Delights Candy - it's just too good to resist!

Word Warp

Now it's Poppet's turn to test her word power! The huggilicious little critter will be monstrously mortified if she doesn't get five outta five. Can you help save her blushes? Read each word, then tick the word underneath it that shares the same meaning.

1. What's another word for CLIMB?
- [ ] FLY
- [ ] ASCEND
- [ ] LEAP
- [ ] CRAWL

2. What's another word for FIELD?
- [ ] MEADOW
- [ ] PARK
- [ ] HILL
- [ ] VALLEY

3. What's another word for SNAKE?
- [ ] EEL
- [ ] BUG
- [ ] SERPENT
- [ ] REPTILE

4. What's another word for RED?
- [ ] INDIGO
- [ ] MAUVE
- [ ] AZURE
- [ ] SCARLET

5. What's another word for DUSK?
- [ ] SUNSET
- [ ] SUNRISE
- [ ] MIDNIGHT
- [ ] DAWN

TYRA'S HIP TIP

Goo York IT-girl, gossip queen, and general mistress of Moshi style, Tyra Fangs, leads the way when it comes to interior design! She inspires the most sophisticated MonSTAR homes in Monstro City.

Today Tyra's got a tip on the latest hot ticket item in fashion-conscious houses. OMM! These collectibles are so now, she can't even say them out loud. Use Tyra's canny letter code to reveal the accessories that you should be spending your hard-earned Rox on!

Cipher key:

A = Φ	N = ◇		
B = □	O = ◉		
C = ▽	P = ∩		
D = ◪	Q = Ω		
E = ✕	R = Л		
F = ‡	S = ⅄		
G = ✳	T = δ		
H = ≡	U = <		
I = ⊣•	V = ⦂		
J = ⊥	W = ✗		
K = ⊠	X = ✱		
L = И	Y = •|•		
M = ⋀	Z = ⟊		

Coded message (decoded):

HORRODS MOSHLING
EGGS ARE THE
MUST-HAVE CRAZE
THIS SEASON!

___ ___ ___ ___ ___ ___ ___

___ ___ ___ ___ ___ ___ ___ ___

___ ___ ___ ___

___ ___ ___ - ___ ___ ___ ___

___ ___ ___ ___ ___

___ ___ ___ ___ ___!

I Can See A Rainbow ...

... ahem, well, sort of. This portrait of expert sky surfer Roy G. Biv has got utterly jumbled in the breeze! Can you bring the rainbows back to Monstro City by carefully creating a new work of art on the opposite page?

Copy each square in the grid below into the matching letter square on the blank grid. It's a doddle, or should we say doodle? When you've re-drawn Mr Biv and his rainbows, colour them in using your brightest colouring pencils!

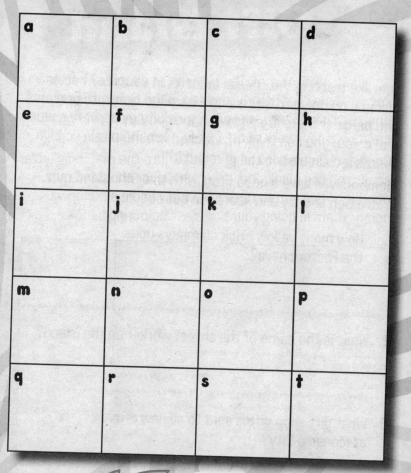

a	b	c	d
e	f	g	h
i	j	k	l
m	n	o	p
q	r	s	t

Better hurry up, Roy G. Biv Day is just around the corner!

Gift Island

Feel like treating the special monster in your life? Better shimmy on down to Gift Island – it's piled high with presents and parcels! There are gift-wrapped goodies in every shape and colour you can think of, stacked in a mountain so high there's a train track running round it!

Members will have a head-start with this Gift Island quiz. Grab a pen and try and score ten out of ten!

1. How many yellow brick chimneys does the Factory have?

....

2. What is the name of the shyest worker on the island?

....

3. What gift shop gift is sent to all new arrivals at Monstro City?

....

4. What colour hands does Clem's RoboDonut have?

....

....

5. Where is the hand that throws gifts towards Monstro City?

....

6. What bobs in the water by the jetty?

....

7. What is Skeeter Rydell's job?

....

8. What creature is perched on the roof of the pink building?

....

9. What colour is Oiler the octopus?

....

10. What connects the two parts of Gift Island?

....

Nice doin' business with ya!

Cha-Ching!

Sly Chance has got a great head for figures – to keep Dodgy Dealz in profit, he has to tot up totals and suss out sales at lightning speed! Could you strike the right bargain each and every time? Step into the shack and find out . . .

1. A Hornament costs 79 Rox. How much will three of them cost?

2. A Baby Diavlo photo originally cost 35 Rox, but Sly only wants to pay 80% of that. How much will he pay?

3. A box of Katsuma Krunch weighs 2kg. How many 400g portions can Sly get from it?

4. Sly has agreed to wait two and a half hours before selling on a pre-loved Cupcake Scare Bear. How many minutes is that?

5. Sly buys a WallScrawl S for 10 Rox, but turns a profit of 100% when he sells it on. How much does it go for?

6. Sly lays his tentacles on a square Stone Fireplace with a perimeter of 45cm. What is the length of each side?

SUPER TOUGH!

Getting Jiggy With It

Tonight the Underground Disco is heaving with Moshis that want to party and no wonder - super group the Moshi MonStars are in town! Get the show on the road, by drawing a line to put the missing jigsaw pieces back into the scene.

a.

b.

c.

d.

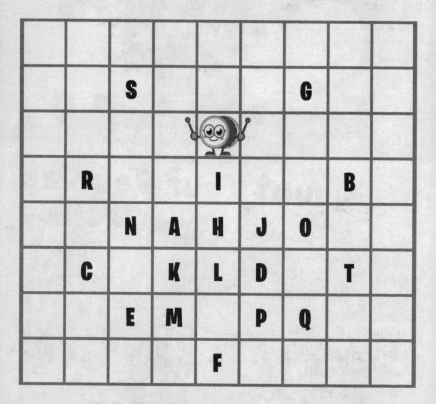

BLOCK PARTY

Some monsters really need to get themselves a sat nav!

Put your finger on the critter in the centre of the grid. Now move him two blocks east, three blocks south, four blocks west and another block south. Where does he end up? Draw a circle around letter marking the monster's destination.

		S				G	
			(monster)				
	R		I			B	
	N	A	H	J	O		
	C	K	L	D		T	
	E	M		P	Q		
		F					

WALL SCRAWL

When monsters pop into Babs' Boutique, they all want to know the secret of the merchant's fangtastic hair. How does Babs get her scarlet quiff looking A1 every single day?

Babs is ready to reveal her secret, but only to those that are smart enough to suss it out. Unjumble the wallscrawl letters and you could have monstrous hair, too!

UBY LORFO HOPSIL RMOF
HET ENEZSE XWA OCAPNMY
DAN SCKIL TI NO!

_ _ _ _ _ _ _ _ _ _ _ _ _ _ _ _ _ _ _

_ _ _ _ _ _ _ _ _ _ _ _ _ _ _ _ _ _ _ !

_ _ _ _ _ _ _ _ _ _ _ _ _ _ _ _ _ _ _

---

140 Count Your Pennies

Heads or tails? This puzzle is packed full of flipping Mini Money Moshlings! See if you can count up how many times Penny's name appears on this page. Better hurry - we wouldn't want one to slip down the side of the sofa!

PENNY PENNY PENNY
PENNY PENNY PENNY
PENNY PENNY PENNY
PENNY PENNY PENNY
PENNY PENNY PENNY
PENNY PENNY

Write your answer in here.

BUSTER'S ALBUM

Greetings, fellow Moshling Hunters! Monstro City's top Moshling Collector, Buster Bumblechops, has decided to give you puzzlers a sneak peek of his family photo album. He's carefully captioned all his snaps, but a cheeky Chop Chop has swung in and mixed up all the labels. Ha-dee-ha! Can you put things right again?

5

6

A I'll do anything to get close to Moshlings. The only way to keep up with Cutie Pie is rocket-powered roller skates!

B Moshlings can pop up in the unlikeliest of places. Sometimes even a leisurely Ginger Snap can take me by surprise.

C This cheeky Tiki nearly made off with my hat!

D Resting up at the end of another very long day!

E I've been chasing Moshlings since I was knee-high to a Snoodle.

F There's no doubt about it – I like Moshlings as much as they like me! These Baby Tumteedums were adorable.

Potty Flowers All In A Row

When it comes to attracting Moshlings, you've just got to get your hands dirty! Planting seeds in crazy combos is the only way to lure the little critters into your garden.

The seed combos on these pages will help you attract eight Moshlings outta the wild. Look at each trio, then write down the species the blooms will attract.

1.

_____

2.

_____

3.

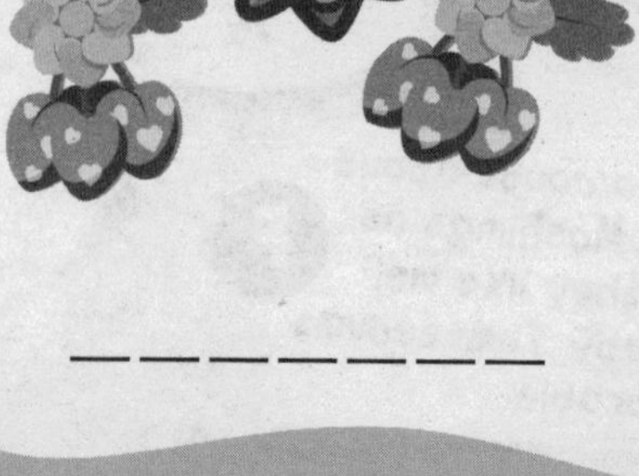

_____

4. _ _ _ _ _ _ _

5. _ _ _ _ _ _

6. _ _ _ _ _ _ _ _ _ _

7. _ _ _ _ _ _ _

8. _ _ _ _ _ _ _

Mixed-up Moshlings

Which trio of Moshlings are hiding in the jumbled jigsaw?

1. ....

2. ....

3. ....

Need a clue? Every one scampers on four little legs!

BANGERS
AND MASH

This famished Furi can't wait to get his fangs into a plate of Bangers and Mash! The Gross-ery Store stocks a drool-worthy new brand that is highly explosive. Be wary! The Glumps have tampered with one of these plates of nosh. Draw a big cross over the odd-one-out.

A.

B.

C.

D.

E.

F.

Crazy Quilt

A stitch in time saves nine, or should that be a stitch in nine is quilt quiz time?

Whatever! Take a peek at my latest quilting project, puzzle fans. Only one of these squares has a tiny flaw in it - can you pick it out from the rest?

A B C

D E F

G H I

Put-Out Pets

This menagerie of Puppies and Kitties are driving Diavlo insane! Why won't these Moshlings stop yapping, yowling and meowing? Study the rows of barking mad mini-mutts and moggies and you'll understand - these pages are packed with pet imposters!

Circle the correct Moshling in each group.

Puppies

Giuseppe Getaway

Monstro City's fave Ice-Scream man, Giuseppe Gelato, has got himself in a frosty fix! He's been so busy running around trying to drum up custom, he's forgotten where he parked his van! Help him find a way back to the Ice-Scream machine, before the crowd decide to help themselves.

Waldo's Wacky Word Box

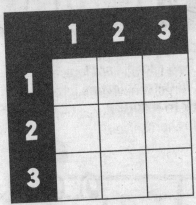

Waldo's back again with another bonkers brainteaser! The Tabby Nerdicat has created a word box where the answer to each clue is filled in across and downwards at the same time. Can you crack it?

CLUES

1. Just a _ _ _
2. Something that surrounds us. _ _ _
3. The opposite of wet. _ _ _

Remember to write each answer across as well as down!

Line Dance

This puzzle is wrigglin' and writhin' with parallel lines! Pore over the page, then count up the total number of separate lines featured.

Write your answer in the box.

Funny Faceword

Yeah, yeah, yeah - you've seen these folks a squillion times, but do you know their names? Take a long, hard look at every Moshi mugshot, then fill the correct letters into the crossword grid. It's a crazy, funny faceword!

Across

1. (8, 7)
2. (4)
3. (6)
4. (5)
5. (5)

Down

1. (3, 7)
2. (5, 3)
3. (7)
4. (3, 3)
5. (4)

Shuffle Kerfuffle

He was billed as THE hottest jazz talent in Monstro City - a cuddly crooner with a taste for rock and roll living! This guy's appetite for caviar cost him his fortune. You've probably seen him with his fishing pole on the jetty at The Port, but what is he called? Unshuffle the letters to find out!

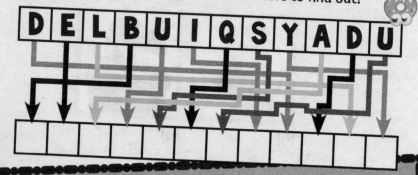

| D | E | L | B | U | I | Q | S | Y | A | D | U |

BIG BAD BILL

No Woolly Blue Hoodoo can resist riddles! These mystic Spookies are intrigued by hexes, spells and word games of every description. Big Bad Bill has used his Staff of Power to summon up these fiendishly difficult riddles for this book. Can you can crack them?

What always runs but never walks, often murmurs, never talks, has a bed but never sleeps, has a mouth but never eats?

....

What is in seasons, seconds, centuries and minutes but not in decades, years or days?

....

D is for Dress Up Room!

Need to glam up for a big monster party? Head into your Dress Up room and get creative!

This monster is back from a stupendous shopping trip to Diavlo's Duds. Now he's flicking through his wardrobe, picking out a smokin' set of glad rags to wear. He's made a list of the items that he's after. Can you find the right accessories to pull the look together?

Glove mitts ☐
(To stop me burning my hands every time I scratch my head!)

Build-a Human Ears ☐
(From a genu-ine Hu-maaan!)

Flamin' shades ☐
(They're sooooo hot!)

Welding Mask ☐
(Great for head-butting walls, too!)

Here Be Monsters

Monstro City sure is an amazing place! Just go on Googley Maps and you'll discover some of the most awesome landscapes ever. No wonder Bushy Fandango and her White Fang Puppies can't stop roaming its snowy mountains, shell-studded beaches and candy encrusted caves!

MONSTRO
City

1.

2.

3.

4.

How much of this monstrous land have you explored?
Carefully label every landmark that you recognize.
Betcha know it like the back of your paw!

5.

6.

7.

8.

TRICKY TEXTS

Gabby is such an up-to-the-minute Mini Moshifone, she never wastes unnecessary characters in her texts! Just a few prods of her touchscreen and she's pinging new messages off, left, right and centre.

Take a look at some of the Techie's abbreviations. What do the numbers and letters stand for? The chatty gadget has done the first one to get you started.

5 F ON A H =

5 fingers on a hand.........................

52 C IN A D =

....

8 P IN THE S S =

....

266 D IN A L Y =

....

11 P IN A F T =

....

26 L IN THE A =

....

SUPER TOUGH

PERVERSE VERSE

Do the lines of this ditty ring any bells?
Read the rhyme, then write the correct
Monster name underneath it.

> I was hit with the ugly stick, true, I'll admit it,
> You can say that I'm freakish, oh yes, I'll permit it,
> But just because I fall apart at the seam,
> Doesn't mean we can't make a top team!

Shape Shake

Shape up, puzzlers, this challenge is up against the clock! Set your stopwatch, Rock Clock or eye-Phone to thirty seconds, then make a dash through the quiz questions below.

A. What is the most common shape on the board?

....

B. How many triangles are there in total?

....

C. What is the shape with six sides called?

....

D. How many shapes are black?

....

MYSTERY MONSTER

Slimy slop buckets, there's another bashful Moshi hiding in the shadows! Read the rhyme, then fill in the name of the mild-mannered monster.

A cuter Moshi you'll struggle to find,

I'm sweeter and smaller than most of my kind.

My eyes are just huge, I wear boots on my feet,

Six whiskers and pink fur, make me so sweet!

Count With Clutch

159

Poor Clutch has got his work cut out today. The dedicated delivery turtle has got so many gifts to deliver to Monster owners, he's had to load the sacks into a van! Help Clutch get across town by counting up the total number of bags crammed into the trailer.

Write the total in here

ANACROSSAGRAM

Check out pop artist Art Lee's unique brand of back-to-front crossword - the Anacrossagram! Find the anagram of each word that fits into the correct place in the grid.

1	2	3	4
2			
3			
4			

Across
1. MOOD
2. LONG
3. LONE
4. PONG

Down
1. POOL
2. GONG
3. LEND
4. MOON

161 Cleverer Than Cleo?

SUPER TOUGH!

Pretty Pyramids were believed extinct, until a sandstorm uncovered a host of them playing in the lost valley of iSissi. Cleo loves to smile and nothing makes her smile wider than riddles! Here are four of her faves - can you crack them?

1. The man who invented it doesn't want it. The man who bought it doesn't need it. The man who needs it doesn't know it. What is it?

2. I'm light as a feather, yet even the strongest man can't hold me for much more than a minute. What am I?

3. What comes once in a minute, twice in a moment, but never in a thousand years?

4. What walks on four legs at first, then on two, then on three?

TECHIE TEST

Hey monster! If you're not goo goo for gadgets, skip over this page. This brain-melting quiz features all the newest Techies in Monstro City and none of 'em come with an instruction manual! Are you savvy enough to score ten out of ten?

1. What does Gabby like most?
a. Eighteen month contracts
b. Mad Moshi texts
c. Monsters that hang up

2. What type of Moshling is Nipper?
a. A Tetchy Trundlebot
b. A Tiny Trundlebot
c. A Titchy Trundlebot

3. Which Techie is the most common?
a. Wurley
b. Gabby
c. Wallop

4. Who are you most likely to find on Shutter Island?
a. A Happy Snappy
b. A Mini Moshifone
c. A Twirly Tiddlycopter

5. What does Wurley love to hum?
a. Hip hop and Monstar rap
b. Rock anthems
c. Classical music

6. What is Nipper's favourite sport?
a. Snooker
b. Basketball
c. Tennis

7. Which Techie freaks at the first drop of rain?
a. Nipper
b. Wurley
c. Holga

8. Where do Mini Moshifones like to recharge?
a. Amp Alley
b. Voltage Vaults
c. Battery Basin

9. Which troupe of Techies once got tricked by Strangeglove?
a. A squadron of Twirly Tiddlycopters
b. A band of Jolly Tubthumpers
c. A team of Titchy Trundlebots

10. What's the name of the Happy Snappy with the little blue lens cap?
a. Heidi
b. Holga
c. Hermione

BBBBBrrringgggg! Did you know that in Japan, people say 'moshi moshi' when they pick up the phone instead of hello...?!

WOMBAT WORD SEARCH

A curious furry Moshling has hi-yaaaed across this page, kicking out words left, right and centre! The naughty Ninja must have rampaged here from Chillybot State Park, a weirdy wasteland of a place where darkness never falls.

The word search opposite is packed with nuggets of Ninja info, but you're gonna have to find the clues as well as the answers! Fill in the blanks on this page, then circle the words in the letter grid.

_ _ _ _ _ _ _ Wombats are a mysterious type of _ _ _ _ _ _ _ _ that were once used to guard _ _ _ _ and other precious things. General _ _ _ _ _ _ and his ilk are said to not need any _ _ _ _ _ at night. Their eyes always seem open, but _ _ _ _ _ _ _ Bumblechops' research has proved this is a sham! He has proved that their vigilant peepers are actually little _ _ _ _ tins welded on to their hats. If you want to attract one of these sleepyheads you'll have to work hard. Red Hot _ _ _ _ _ Peppers, _ _ _ _ Berries and Star _ _ _ _ _ _ _ might tempt the Moshling into your garden.

```
F U Z U K I A R K J L W
D I F A M A G H B T V L
Q Z B L O S S O M M K O
G G R F G E T Y B Q P V
J M T W R Z G B U F Z E
F C Y B Z O N D S M K S
F A X L C D I S T I X D
T K C B L Y L R E O B G
D E D L R I H T R P R H
I D P E E L S C Q A T H
H B J T F G O V M E W Y
C S H W Y V M D X A O O
```

FLAG FRENZY

During his epic voyages Cap'n Buck has sailed the seventy seas, climbed every mountain and explored every corner of the Monstrosphere, but even HE needs some help picking out his Tricolores from his Union Jacks.

These country flags are each missing their identifying colours. Study each one, then write down the shades needed.

SWEDEN

....
....
....

JAMAICA

....
....
....

FRANCE

....
....
....

CHINA

....
....
....

MATHS MASH

MATHS MASH IS MY FAVOURITE GAME IN THE PUZZLE
PALACE. NOW IT IS YOUR TURN TO SHARPEN YOUR PENCIL
AND GET CALCULATING. JUST FILL THE MISSING DIGITS AND
SYMBOLS INTO EACH OF THE TROUBLESOME SUMS.

SUPER TOUGH!

a. 78 ___ 12 = 936

b. 85 - ___ = 22

c. 26 x 8 = ___

d. 355 ÷ ___ = 71

e. 739 ___ 478 = 1217

f. 1452 + ___ = 2241

g. 188 ___ 5 = 37.6

h. ___ x 58 = 1914

Shape Shake

Shape up, puzzlers, this challenge is up against the clock! Set your stopwatch, Rock Clock or eye-Phone to thirty seconds, then make a dash through the quiz questions below.

1. What is the most common shape on the board?

....

2. How many triangles are there in total?

....

3. What is the five-sided shape called?

....

4. How many shapes are black?

....

Spooky Sudoku

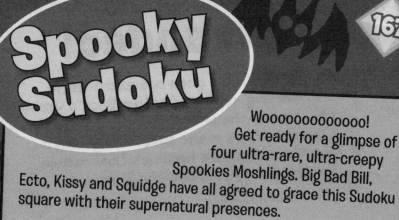

Wooooooooooooo!
Get ready for a glimpse of four ultra-rare, ultra-creepy Spookies Moshlings. Big Bad Bill, Ecto, Kissy and Squidge have all agreed to grace this Sudoku square with their supernatural presences.

Can you draw in more Spookies to fill up the Sudoku grid? Make sure each of the four Moshlings feature once only in each row, column and four by four box.

Stranded!

Oh no! The tide's gone out extra-early this morning, leaving Captain Buck's vessel beached on the shore! Now the *Cloudy Cloth Clipper* is stuck in the sand, along with a handful of hapless hearties. Unscramble the letters to find out who they are.

LIGA

YENLN RLDA

DESTLID

YLIBL BBO ABANMIT

RM WODFRMOE

It's a right sorry tale, that it is!

Tricky Trivia

Howdy-doody, what have we here? Yep, it's another general knowledge romp against the clock! Set your timer to thirty seconds, then tick the correct answer to each triv challenge.

1. Who was the monarch before Queen Elizabeth II?
- ☐ KING GEORGE IV
- ☐ KING GEORGE III
- ☐ QUEEN VICTORIA
- ☐ KING GEORGE V

2. What's the capital city of Scotland?
- ☐ DUNDEE
- ☐ ABERDEEN
- ☐ EDINBURGH
- ☐ GLASGOW

3. If it's five months since Christmas, what month is it?
- ☐ MARCH
- ☐ MAY
- ☐ JULY
- ☐ AUGUST

4. What is the largest continent in the world?
- ☐ AUSTRALASIA
- ☐ EUROPE
- ☐ AFRICA
- ☐ ASIA

5. How many players are there in a cricket team?
- ☐ 12
- ☐ 11
- ☐ 8
- ☐ 6

Eyes Spy

Jeepers creepers, where'dya get those peepers? Ken Tickles has got three of the weirdest ones in Monstro City! The grumpy Roarker has drilled up a few more eyeballs to keep you entertained – can you count them all?

Write the total in this box.

Dear Diary

Roving music reporter Ruby Scribblez is a rock and roll chick from the top of her tousled purple mane to the bottom of her high-fashion heels! She's used to brushing horns with celebs, but today even she's maxed out. After a busy day in showbiz land, Ruby's ready to dish!

Fill in the blanks to hear all the deets of Ruby's day.

Dear Diary,

What an awesome day – I lurrrrve writing for _ _ _ _ _ _ _ _ _ _ Magazine!

When I got to my desk, one of my most trusted Fluffy sources, _ _ _ _ _, called to say that teen sensation _ _ _ _ Binspin had been spotted sipping bug juice in Ooh _ _ Lane!

Naturally I skedaddled right over there with Holga the _ _ _ _ _ Snappy, primed and ready to shoot!

The minute we arrived, the day just got even better! First Mr Binspin posed for some top pix, then he introduced us to his celebrity friend _ _ _ _ _ LeScream from the _ _ _ _ _ _ _!

OMM!!!!! The two stars were totally divine - in fact, the three of us got on like a house on fire. Just as we were swapping digits, the rest of the band cruised by. Result?

Three tickets to see them play at the Underground _ _ _ _ _.

The band totally rocked, as did we! At the end, me and the stars made a date to meet at the same time next week. Yowzers!!!

Ruby Scribblez

Bubble Trouble

I've been huffing and puffing all day to get this extreme bubble brain challenge ready for you! Study the bubbles carefully. Can you get every question correct without muddling your mind?

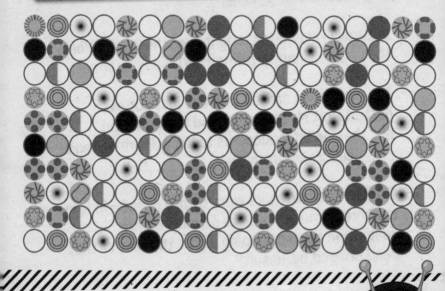

1. How many bubbles have four spots? ....

2. There are twice as many black bubbles than white bubbles? True or false? ....

3. How many bubbles are there?...........................

4. One bubble is different from the rest of its group. Can you find it?...

SUPER TOUGH!

Squidge Squish

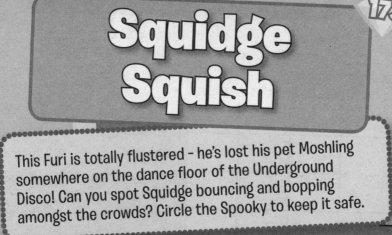

This Furi is totally flustered - he's lost his pet Moshling somewhere on the dance floor of the Underground Disco! Can you spot Squidge bouncing and bopping amongst the crowds? Circle the Spooky to keep it safe.

ANACROSSAGRAM

Check out another of pop artist Art Lee's amazing Anacrossagrams! Find the anagram of each word that fits into the correct place in the grid.

1	2	3	4
2			
3			
4			

Across
1. SASH
2. LASH
3. OMEN
4. OGRE

Down
1. GOSH
2. HARM
3. LOAN
4. SEES

Remember in this quiz, the letters can be arranged in any order - no sense required!

NIFTY SHIFTY

The stone head outside the Volcano is a stickler for rules - if your name's not down, you're certainly not coming in to the Super Moshi's HQ! Although he's ancient, the Gatekeeper hasn't always been on duty in Monstro City. Shift the letters to find out where he used to reside.

Move each letter back three places to crack the puzzle.

KH RQFH WRSSHG WKH WDOOHVW WRWHP SROH LQ WLNNLKDDKDD

-- ---- ------ --- ------- -----

---- -- -----------

MonSTAR Mirror

Tyra Fangs never tires of gazing into her dress-up room mirror! Today however, something seems to have gone awry. Ms Banks' lovely looks have got weirdly distorted - could Strangeglove be up to no good?

Peer into the looking glass, then circle six differences between Tyra and her reflection.

Batty Boxes

Blurp spends his time swimming in circles and looking at things without taking them in. He's all puffed up with nowhere to blow! Can you do any better? Each of these boxed puzzles hides a saying, place or common catchphrase. Don't just read the letters, think about how they're placed.

1.
```
B  B  B  B
A  A  A  A
R  R  R  R
G  G  G  G
```

2. W1h1i1l1e

3.
packTHINGSages
packTHINGSages
packTHINGSages

4. TORE
TOE

5. DR
EAMS

6. SDRAW

Whirly Worldies

Wow, those Worldies really do get around!
Three species of these monu-mental Moshlings
are having a ball at the Fun Park. Only one
is conspicuously absent. Can you circle the
thrillseekers, then work out who's missing?

WHO AM I?

Which gooey, green Moshi citizen do these clues describe?

SUPER TOUGH!

1. I'm sticky, I'm gloopy, but I'm bubbly too.

2. I'm training to become a blimp at next year's Moshi Carnival.

3. I'm a world-record holder at holding my breath.

4. I can be found in the tunnels beneath Monstro City.

I'm _ _ _ _ _ _ _ _ _ _ !

Tricky Trivia

It's never trivial to test your trivia! Can you correctly answer these five culture-based questions, set by amateur artist Art Lee? There's just one catch - you've only got thirty seconds to crack them all . . .

1. Who painted the Mona Lisa?

☐ MONET
☐ DA VINCI
☐ VAN GOGH
☐ PICASSO

2. What is the name of the lion in the book *The Lion, the Witch and the Wardrobe*?

☐ MR TUMNUS
☐ ASLAN
☐ NARNIA
☐ ARAGOG

3. Which famous composer was deaf?

☐ BACH
☐ WAGNER
☐ BEETHOVEN
☐ MOZART

4. Which author created Tracy Beaker?

☐ JACQUELINE WILSON
☐ J K ROWLING
☐ JULIA DONALDSON
☐ FRANCESCA SIMON

5. Which of these plays was not written by William Shakespeare?

☐ *TWELFTH NIGHT*
☐ *ROMEO & JULIET*
☐ *AS YOU LIKE IT*
☐ *DR FAUSTUS*

Dear Agony Ant...

There's never a dull day in Monstro City! Luckily Agony Ant is always on hand to offer her wisdom when there's a Moshi or Moshling in need of advice. Have a rummage through the fortune-teller's postbag, then write the correct names underneath each letter.

LETTER A

Dear Agony,

I'm writing in because I set up two of my friends on a date that went disastrously wrong – they didn't get on at all! Now one of them won't even talk to me. She says I should butt out and stop getting involved, but I know I'm totally A.MAZE.ING at matchmaking. Should I apologise or just say like, what-ever! Also, why can't I find anyone myself when (like hello!!!)
I'm so gorge and cute, Fishies must be totally crushing on me all the time . . .

....

Dear Ms Ant,

I own a store on Ooh La Lane and the customer footfall is so great that I have to take on part-time staff. The trouble is that many of them don't work quickly enough, so my customers get fed up and leave! I am worried that my store will get a bad reputation. What should I do?

Dear AA,

My boyfriend and I have had a role reversal recently and it's beginning to affect our relationship. I used to work in Goo York as a model, but then I moved to Monstro City to be with my boyf. For a long time all I did was shop and have facials, but with so much spare time on my hands I was turning into one bossy babe! Now I've set up my own spa and am loving owning my own business, but my other half is resenting the fact I don't have so much time to devote to him. How do we fix this?

Still foxed? Here are some freebie anagram clues to help you. You don't even have to cross my palm with silver!

RATY NAGSF   **CAIL**   **IGUPEEPS GOATEL**

Binspin Doodle

Swooooon! He's the Moptop Tweenybop that sets pulses racing among the Moshis. Can you bring the heartthrob to life by copying his gorgeous face square by square into the empty grid?

Sketch carefully - don't mess up the hair!

A

B

C

D

E

F

G

I

H

J

K

L

EYES SPY

SUPER TOUGH!

Eye eye, it's another extreme puzzle!
This brainbuster has been set by Sly Chance, a Moshi who always wants to see the whites of your eyes when he's doing a deal (even though he'll never show you his).

Carefully tot up the eyeballs. Write the total in this box.

Sack the Stylist!

Miss Preen
MAGAZINE

Mizz's beauty secrets

FREE gloop facemask!

Oooh! The latest ish of Miss Preen Magazine has hit the news stands of Monstro City, but it looks like there's been a monstrous printing error. Which beauty queen's features have been jumbled up on the front cover?

---

185 Master of Moshi

What is this peculiar object known as?

An Octowent ☐

A Tentacle Chair ☐

A Fishy Fez ☐

An Eight-Arm ☐

Billy Bob's Boots

Heave ho, me hearties! Avid fisherman Billy Bob Baitman is famous for his catches, but nothing he seems to snag on his line ever has scales or fins. Can you count up how many boots Billy's caught to date?

Write the number here. ☐

SUPER TOUGH!

MOSHI MARATHON

When they get in the zone, Moshi Monsters can be very competitive! Recently there was a marathon in Monstro City to raise funds for charity - almost every Beastie in town turned out to have a go. Can you use logic to work out who the final finishers were? What place did they each achieve?

Katsuma came third and Poppet came second. Luvli, Diavlo and Zommer all passed the finishing line, too.

Luvli was not last.   Zommer was not first.

Luvli came in after Poppet.

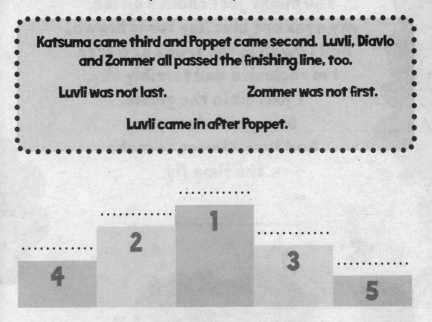

Only one slouchy Moshi Monster couldn't be bothered to pull on his trainers and get running.
Who was it?

Super-Furry Animal

Sshh! There's a tiny critter hiding behind the shadow on this page. If the spilled splotches of berry juice don't give away his identity, maybe this poem will . . .

If you go down to the woods today,
You might just chance on me,
My eyes are blue, my fur is brown,
And I dwell in the trunk of a tree.
I'm reclusive and terribly shy,
I just sit in the gloom,
Of my circular room,
And type stories to make
the time fly.

SUPER TOUGH!

Waldo's Wacky Word Box

	1	**2**	**3**
1			
2			
3			

Wowee! It's another one of Waldo's wacky word boxes. The answer to each clue is filled in both across and down the grid - can you crack it in less than fifteen seconds?

Remember to write each answer across as well as down!

CLUES

1. Possess. _ _ _
2. Small. _ _ _
3. The divider on a tennis court. _ _ _

ANACROSSAGRAM

Pop Artist extraordinaire Art Lee just can't get enough of these Anacrossagrams - the mad Moshi take on the crossword. All you've got to do is write the clues into the grid. It doesn't matter what order you put the letters in as long as they fit both across and down.

Across
1. REIN
2. DEED
3. DEER
4. DUAL

Down
1. DEAD
2. NUDE
3. RIDE
4. LEER

1	2	3	4
2			
3			
4			

Are you brave enough to take on the Warrior Wombat's numerical test? Each letter of the alphabet in the grid below has been given a value between 1 and 26. General Fuzuki has been generous and has already entered some of the answers. Your mission, should you choose to accept it, is to work out the value of each of the remaining letters! Most of these have an arithmetic clue shown in the middle tier of the grid, but some have no clue at all - you'll need all your powers of reasoning to work them out. Happy number hunting!

Symbol key:
- **+** plus
- **-** minus
- **/** divided by
- **x** multiplied by
- **>** more than
- **<** less than

SUPER TOUGH!

A	B	C	D	E	F	G	H	I	J	K	L	M
HxW	Q-T	>V	T-L		Bx2	I+J	F/N	E+N	K+T		H-E	Q+E
			2							16	4	

N	O	P	Q	R	S	T	U	V	W	X	Y	Z
	>Q	E+U	C-W	ExS	L+N	F-N	L+J		<N		G+L	>D
6							17			20		

The Curse of IGGY

IGGY, the Ultra Rare Pixel-Munching Moshling, loves filling his face with computer cursors! Today he's chanced upon a veritable banquet of arrows. Can you count how many he can crunch on this page?

Pssst! Did you know that IGGY actually finds cursors rather irksome. As he doesn't have any arms or legs to bat them away, eating 'em is his only option!

SIMON SAYS...

Simon Growl is judging a screech-off between Max Volume, Clem and Zack Binspin. His scorecards will give the contestants a mark from one to ten.

Read the statements below, then work out each of the screecher's scores and write them on Simon's boards. Which contestant won?

SUPER TOUGH!

Max Volume's score is half of sixteen multiplied by three, minus seventeen

Zack Binspin's score is two less than Max's score, added to Clem's score.

Clem's score is half of Max's score, minus one and a half, multiplied by two.

chock-a-block

Sneaky Tiki the Pilfering Toucan has been 'borrowing' things for his nest again. The bold Birdie's been pinching blocks and stacking them up, ready to drag away. How many blox has he hoarded so far?

SUPER TOUGH!

Write your answer in here.

Elusive Egg Head

One type of Uncommon Moshling is totally OTT about the threat of Killer Canaries, but which is it? Read the rhyme then use your masterful Moshi knowledge to write their name underneath.

My headgear's fragile,
But it's MINE,
It's for protection,
And looks fine!
No other Dino,
Can compare,
Don't ask to borrow,
I don't share!

My name is . . .

....

THE DRILL

Ken Tickles is hard at work - he's on a schedule to lay five brand new pipes! Unfortunately Ken's lazy co-worker Bjorn Squish hasn't done the required testing and has now gone to lunch, practically inviting several cheeky Moshlings to take up residence in the newly dug holes.

Can you pick the only section of ground that is still safe for Ken to drill?

Loopy Line-Up

These batty Moshlings are all one Barfmallow short of a picnic! Each one has lost something important, but they're too daft to work out what! Check out the loony list, then try and spot the odd Moshling out in each line.

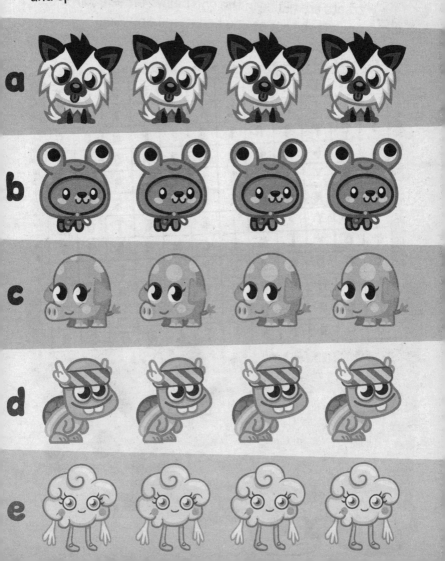

Gross-Out Wordsearch

Yummy, yummy in my Monster's tummy! Can you track down the delicious delicacies currently on offer chez Snozzle Wobbleson? Ten gulp-tastic treats are hiding in the grid below. Cross each one off the list as you find it – no dribbling!

A	S	L	U	D	G	E	F	U	D	G	E
B	L	I	W	D	U	F	U	F	E	S	G
I	U	P	B	R	L	B	F	F	R	O	G
L	G	G	A	D	O	S	D	A	O	T	P
I	G	Y	J	O	L	I	E	T	A	S	L
H	O	N	A	U	L	B	T	D	S	A	A
C	E	Y	E	P	I	E	Y	E	T	O	N
Y	O	Y	L	M	P	C	M	E	B	R	T
L	O	O	M	R	L	P	E	N	E	W	K
L	S	U	Y	V	O	S	Y	P	A	L	O
I	C	R	X	H	P	F	D	O	S	H	O
S	L	O	P	N	I	T	A	W	T	S	H

BUG JUICE
EGG PLANT
EYE PIE
LOLLIPLOP
ROAST BEAST

SCUMMI BEARS
SILLY CHILI
SLOP
SLUDGE FUDGE
TOAD SODA

PRINT PANIC

There's panic in the Print Workshop! Last night Sweet Tooth broke in, ransacking the joint in a sugar-fuelled candy rampage. Before disappearing back into the starlight, the baddie also muddled up the colouring sheets. Label the Moshi body parts so that the pictures can be put back together again.

VOWEL HOWL

Can you holler and howl like a beastie? Burnie and Jeepers yelp with delight at the very sight of these vowel-based puzzles!

- ☐ **GOAT**
- ☐ **GASH**
- ☐ **SAND**
- ☐ **SITE**

Which of these words has all of its vowels in the same position as the word below? Tick the right box.

GAME

The Stuff of Legends

Today Colonel Catcher has decided to take a break from Flutterby hunting. Who has he set his sights on instead?

SUPER TOUGH!

Extra clue:
This blue bather is a legend in his own lunchtime. He also has a surprisingly tuneful voice!

Got it? Now earn yourself extra Moshi merits by retelling the legend that surrounds this incredible character.

....

....

....

....

Cloud Jumping

Roy G. Biv takes extreme Moshi sportsmanship to a new level! Can you work out which cloud path he will have to surf to get from Kaleido Island to Monstro City? The rules say he can only stay on clouds where the answer to the puzzle is an odd number. He can't skip over clouds either.

KALEIDO ISLAND

MONSTRO CITY

8 - 4 =	46 x 4 =	46 x 3 -129 =	111 x 3 - 324 =	12 x 26 - 8 =
19 - 9 =	18 ÷ 2 =	√4 =	52 - 20 + 8 =	53 x 7 - 362 =
12 - 3 =	15 x 6 =	88 ÷ 4 =	87 ÷ 2 x 7 - 2.5 =	22 x 16 ÷ 2 =
36 ÷ 2 =	√25 =	976 - 12 =	57 ÷ 3 =	46 + 88 =
87 + 5 =	86 + 18 =	17 x 20 =	200 x 10 =	2 ÷ 4 x 2 =

SUPER TOUGH!

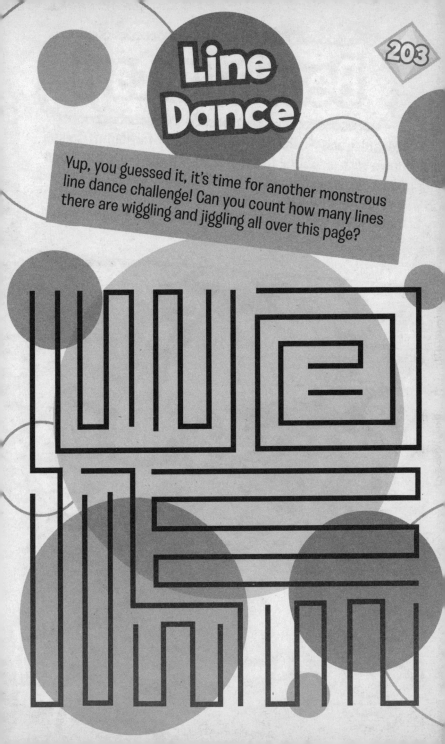

Line Dance

203

Yup, you guessed it, it's time for another monstrous line dance challenge! Can you count how many lines there are wiggling and jiggling all over this page?

Beach Partay!

Monsters and Moshlings love to let their fur/flames/spikes down with an outing to the beach. The Spookies are much more at home in scary surroundings, but even they make an exception for a day by the waves. Can you spot Ecto on the sand? You'll need to look carefully, he's almost translucent.

EYES SPY

Egon Groanay was about to chow down on one of his fave dishes - Eye Pie, but unfortunately the filling has spurted out all over the place! Can you count how many eyeballs are splattered across the page?

Write the total in this box

Ginger Whinger

Gingersnap's at it again - he's a Kitty with issues! Can you suss out what the Whinger Cat's moaning about now? Cross out the first letter and then every third letter of the coded message below to discover what the matter might be.

LFEGED UME XCHIEENSEG OR YFEHEL SMYT WROATVH

____ __ _____ __ ____ __ _____

TEAM A
CASPER AND SKEETER

TEAM B
STOMPER AND CHOMPER

TEAM C
BUBBA AND DIZZY BOLT

Elmore's Conundrum

Uh-oh! Elmore, the biggest Monster in Monstro City has fallen over again, blocking the Grub Truck's path into town. Which team of kind-hearted citizens can find a way to reach him?

TEAM D
BERT AND BUSHY
FANDANGO

Why So Glump?

Those spherical baddies are always lurking in the shadows - waiting to round up Moshlings and deliver them to their master, the naughty Dr. Strangeglove.

When navigating the Monstroverse, it helps to know exactly who, or what you're dealing with. Can you match each Glump on the left to their distinguishing feature on the right?

Roary Scrawl's a workaholic, but his desk is such a mess it's surprising he can even put pen to paper! The two pictures below show him before and after he got up to make himself a cup of bug juice. Can you circle six other things that have mysteriously gone missing?

SCARE SQUARES

No Monster is more rock 'n' roll than Avril LeScream, lead singer of the Moshi MonStars. And what do rock 'n' rollers hate more than anything? Squares! Avril would detest this puzzle on sight, but can you cope with it? Count up many squares are shown below.

SUPER TOUGH!

JEEPERS CREEPERS . . .

. . . where d'ya get those peepers? A cat's eyes are always the first thing you see in the dark. How many pairs of peepers can you spot in the Barmi Swarmi jungle foliage?

There's another beastie hiding here too - can you tell which, just from its eyes?

Write your answer here.

....

Horrods SHOPPING SPLURGE

EXIT

Horrods

They don't let just anyone in, you know! Horrods is the most upmarket store in the whole of Monstro City. The items sold by super-snooty sales girl Mizz Snoots really are a cut above the res

How often do you pop into the top shop in town? Find out if you remember which of these designer items are pricey and which ar going for a song. Join each object up to its correct price tag.

103 Rox   75 Rox   117 Rox   55 Rox

153 Rox   97 Rox   351 Rox

Got 'em all? Sheesh, Mizz Snoots should be paying you!

STOP PRESS!

Some of the vowel keys on Ruby Scribblez's computer have stopped working. Now she's mistyped several stories for the latest Moshi MonStars fanzine – disastro! Can you guess what each headline or news story should say? You'll have to hurry, she's about to go to press!

Moshi MonStars ann££nce W£rld T££r. Zack B£nsp£n to s£pport.

MOSHI MONSTARS T£ KICK £FF T£UR WITH INTIM£T£ GIG £T UND£RGR£UND DISC£ – GU£ST LIST £NLY

V£N SL£P VS DEM£NST£ IN BIG B£ND BUST-UP

R£ckers the M£shi M£nStars were inv£lved in £ mighty music mish£p when £xl V£n Sl£p £ccident£lly dr£pped DJ Dem£nst£'s decks when unl££ding the t£ur bus bef£re their gig £t the legend£ry Fireb£wl l£st night. The K£tsum£ refused t£ t£ke the bl£me f£r dr£pping them, suggesting that Dem£nst£'s mucky ways me£nt they were dripping in T££d S£d£ £nd slipped from his gr£sp!

Whose Hobby Is It Anyway?

All work and no play makes Moshis dull monsters, so instead they fill their downtime with the zaniest pastimes ever! Can you match the Moshi personalities with their fave hobbies? Choose from the list, then write in the spaces below each picture.

BUBBA

1..............................

HOBBIES

Reading back issues of *Hammer Times*
Knitting
Working on robotic donut rigs
Chomping Spider Lollies in one bite
Practicing moves on a Dance, Dance Roarvolution machine
Weightlifting
Listening to Hop-Hop music
Sipping Slug Slurp Slushies

DIZZY BOLT

1..............................

2..............................

ART LEE

1..............................

DEWI

1..............................

2..............................

CLEM

1..............................

2..............................

Mixed-Up Moshlings

These new Moshling kids on the block are
in a right old state. Can you unmuddle them
in your mind and write down their names?
Now add an extra fact about them in the
spaces below.

1.
Nipper
He plays good
music.

2.
Cherry bom
He likes to
EXPLODE!

3.
Tiamo
she bounces

Myrtle
Treasure Diving

Myrtle's been diving for treasure. Can you name the items she's brought up from the murky depths of Potion Ocean?

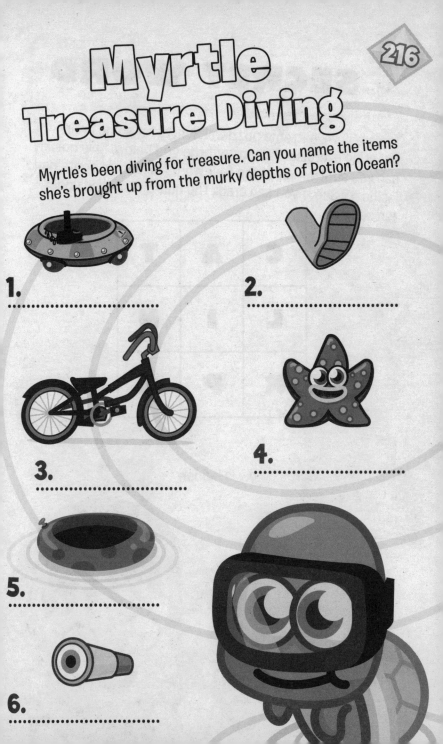

1.
....

2.
....

3.
....

4.
....

5.
....

6.
....

SECRET WORD

Tamara here, extreme puzzlers! Hungry for some brain-boosting exercises? Check out the grid below. How quickly can you spot which of the four words below are contained inside it? See if you can crack the quiz question in under ten seconds.

C	A	T
L	I	N
K	P	A

Which of the words below is hidden in the grid?

APE ☐   KIT ☑

COT ☐   ANT ☐

Moshling-tastic!

Moshlings, don't ya just love those itty-bitty pets for your monster? How many of the darling Moshlings are crowded below?

SUPER TOUGH!

If Your Name's Not Down, You Ain't Comin' In!

Grab a watch and give yourself thirty seconds to drink in the details of this pap snap of nightclub-bouncer/tattoo-artist, Bubba. Now cover the image and see if you can answer these quiz questions.

1. What does Bubba have on his right temple?

Scar scratch thing

2. Bubba wears a white shirt.
☑ True ☐ False

3. Whose name is tattooed on his left arm?

Mom

4. Which tattoo design is highest up his right arm?

Cobweb

5. Bubba has an anchor tattooed onto his wrist.
☐ True ☑ False

6. Bubba has two downward pointing fangs.
☐ True ☑ False

Line Dance

All Moshis love to boogie, but here's a different kind of dance altogether. Can you work out exactly how many lines are housed on this page? Stare with care! If you gawp at the puzzle for too long you'll see more flashing lights than a Saturday night at the Underground Disco.

How many separate ones can you pick out?

FIND THE FLUFFLE

This cute Rummaging Plotamus is happily doing her thang, rummaging for Fluffles in Friendly-Tree Woods. Which path should Doris follow to find her beloved licorice-scented toadstools?

A

B

C

D

Ninja Quiz

Everybody loves Kung Fu fighting! If you find yourself in hot water however, don't count on the Ninjas to get you out of trouble, they're useless against a gang of angry Glumps! Use this quiz to test your Ninja know-how.

1. What does Shelby most dislike?

a. Alarm clocks ☐
b. Jogging ☐
c. Massages ☐

2. What type of Moshling is General Fuzuki?

a. A Warrior Wombat ☐
b. A Furry Fighter ☐
c. A Wacky Woozle ☐

3. What might Chop Chop leave in his wake?

a. Whoopee cushions and stinkbombs ☐
b. Chopped up chunks of Barfmallows ☐
c. A trail of twigs and leaves ☐

4. Which Ninja wears a red bandana?

a. Shelby ☐
b. Sooki-Yaki ☐
c. Chop Chop ☐

5. Which Ninja hibernates under the boardwalk at Groan Bay?

a. General Fuzuki ☐
b. Chop Chop ☐
c. Shelby ☐

6. How much sleep does General Fuzuki need?

a. None ☐
b. About twenty-three hours a day ☐
c. Forty winks once a week ☐

7. To catch Chop Chop you need to plant

a. Magic beans (any), black magic beans and hot silly peppers (any) ☐
b. Magic beans (any), Dragon Fruit (any) and Black Dragon Fruit ☐
c. Three Dragon Fruit (any) ☐

8. Which group of Ninjas are the rarest?

a. Warrior Wombats ☐
b. Caped Assassins ☐
c. Cheeky Chimps ☐

9. According to legend where did Ninja Moshlings once live ?

a. The land of the Surprising Sun ☐
b. Big Toe-kyo ☐
c. Goo York ☐

10. Which skill links Ninjas together?

a. The ability to vanish and reappear ☐
b. The ability to speak Moshlingese ☐
c. The ability to eat their body weight in Spicy Dragon Rolls ☐

Flag Frenzy

Epic explorer Bushy Fandango has spent years of her life mapping out the snowy wilds of the Monstroverse, but she's not so au fait with warmer climes. How about you?

The exotic countries below are shown with their national flags. Each flag is missing its identifying colours. Can you write down the shades needed to make them all complete?

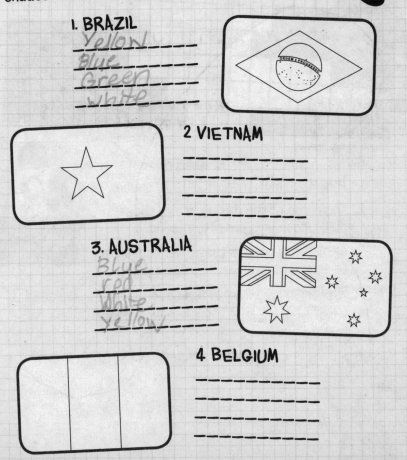

1. BRAZIL
- Yellow
- Blue
- Green
- white

2 VIETNAM
- _____
- _____
- _____
- _____

3. AUSTRALIA
- Blue
- red
- White
- yellow

4 BELGIUM
- _____
- _____
- _____
- _____

Foodie Letter Link

There's a rather charming little Foodie hiding behind this word puzzle. Who could it be? Crack the clues, then read down the highlighted column to find out!

golly

sun

Clues:

1. This Moshling's favourite fruity sauce.

2. The name of the desert where these chilly Moshlings are often found.

3. At birthday parties these Moshlings love to sing 'Freeze a _ _ _ _ _ good fellow'.

4. This Moshling's type is a Magical _ _ _ _ _ _ _ _ _ _.

5. You'll need these seeds in black to catch this Moshling.

6. The type of weather this Moshling detests.

CRASH, BANG, WALLOP!

No one fancies sharing their pad with Wallop! The Jolly Tubthumper is a dedicated drummer - thrashing so loudly he can be heard for miles. The Tunie goes through drumsticks at a rate of 100 pairs a day. How many broken sticks can you count on this page?

Write your answer in here.

Safety First

The Moshis want you as their new recruit at En-Gen, Monstro City's power plant. Chief En-Geneer Dizzy Bolt has turned up to find out if you're trained and ready to roark! Read through the list and put a tick or cross in the box next to each safety rule.

☐	ONLY THREE ROARKERS IN THE EN-GEN ROOM AT A TIME
☐	ALWAYS WEAR A HARD HAT
☐	IN AN EMERGENCY WAIT OUTSIDE FOR THE MONSTRO-ROLE CALL
☐	IN AN EMERGENCY - FLEE
☐	DO NOT ALLOW THE POWER TANK TO EMPTY
☐	DO NOT ALLOW THE POWER TANK TO FILL ABOVE THE RED LINE
☐	CONNECT AND SWAP PLUGS TO GENERATE ENERGY
☐	CONNECT BLOCKS TO GENERATE ENERGY
☐	THE UNIT OF POWER IN MONSTROCITY IS THE MONSTR-AMP

?

DANGER

SUPER TOUGH!

A Day To Remember

Greetings, young ones! There are lots of celebrations and festivals and in the Monstroverse - Halloween is my favourite - I just can't get enough of that Pumpkin Chowder! Let's see how much you know about the MonSTAR calendar.
Can you get six out of six?

1. What do the Monsters and Moshlings celebrate on 25th December?

....

2. Which national holiday occurs on 22nd April?

....

3. When is Roy G. Biv Day and what happens on it?

....

4. Unjumble these letters to name the day when nothing is as it seems. IWYTSCH

....

5. What does Growly Grub Day commemorate?

....

6. Which item can you purchase from the market place on the fourth Thursday of November every year?

....

Sand Shapes

Cleo chills out by making massive sandcastles - this time she's truly outdone herself! The artistic Worldie has created stunning sand sculptures of her fave Moshling pals. Name each one, then list their type and the category that they belong to.

1. Squine
   Sparkies

2. Burnie
   Dino

3. Gabbie
   Techie

4. Mcnulty
   Puppys

5. Peppy
   Birdies

6. Scamp
   Puppies

Crazy Quilt

Flumpy the Pluff is a real homemaker! He loves nothing better than the whiff of rubber gloves and furniture polish. It's no wonder then that this chilled out Moshling is keen on my EXTREME quilting puzzles.

Only one of these squares has a tiny flaw in it - can you help Flumpy locate it?

A

B

C

D

E

F

G

H

I

Sooki-Yaki

Now you see them . . . now you still see them. These Caped Assassins really don't have the element of surprise sussed! Sooki-Yakis have the ability to vanish and re-appear in an instant, but they haven't worked out how to control their power. How many of these Moshlings have popped up in the gardens of Simon Growl's mansion?

Write your answer in here. 19

MUDDLED·UP MOSHLINGS

Colonel Catcher always makes sure the Flutterbies he nets are properly catalogued and labelled. Can you match the anagrams on this page to the six cute Moshling specimens below. Label them properly underneath.

1. *stanley*
2. *purdy*
3. *Humphrey*
4. *cutie pie*
5. *Snookums*
6.

MUKOSONS
YTALNES
HREUPYHM
RUDYP
EPI TIEUC
KIIT

Ooh La Lane Quiz

It's the destination of choice for the sophisticated Monster shopper. From the stylish furnishings of Tyra's Spa to the super-pricey New Houses store,

1. **What red item is lying on the table in the Print Workshop?**

   ....

2. **What revolves on the roof of Giuseppe's store?**

   ....

3. **What building is opposite Tyra's Spa?**

   ....

4. **When viewed from the Monstro City map, what feature runs next to the Moshi Store?**

   ....

5. What creature sleeps on the wall near the Help Kiosk?

....

7. What do you do if you jump in the elevator at the Googenheim?

....

6. What happens if you click on the fountain on Ooh La Lane?

....

8. What does Tyra have outside her spa?

....

BLOCK PARTY

The Katsuma in the centre of the grid is doing a spot of Monster-ienteering. Can you give him a helping finger? Put your pinkie on the Moshi. Now move him three blocks south, one block west and another block north. Where does he end up? Draw a circle around the letter marking his destination.

M	X	B	U	F		
D	O	R	W	I		
L	G		Z	A		
	Q	T	E			
	C	N	J			

Make Your Moshi Mind Up!

Gilbert Finnster has found that someone - probably a mischievous Glump - has torn out a description from the encyclopedia he's writing about Moshlings. Some words have been erased, too. The scrap of paper is such a mess, poor Finnster can't even remember which Moshling he was describing. Help him choose between Gurgle, General Fuzuki, Gigi, Gingersnap and Gabby.

G is for _____Gabby_____

These musical Moshlings can often be heard humming fairground tunes. They love ballroom dancing and making beautiful daisy chains, but can't stand the smell of pickled onions. Incredibly, they can create rainbows beloved of rainbow rider Roy G. Biv. The most interesting fact of all about this Moshling is that a part of its body (its ____Donuts____) is actually edible. If it ever gets munched off, it simply regrows another one.

Psst - do you know what the edible body part of this Moshling is actually made of?

Gruesome Grid

V is for vampire, G is for ghoul and W is for werewolf. Cross out all the Vs, Ws and Gs in this grid to discover the name of another freaky Moshi character.

V	V	W	G	G	W	V	W	W	G
V	G	W	G	V	G	W	G	G	W
G	W	O	G	W	V	G	W	W	G
G	G	W	W	W	G	V	G	W	G
V	E	V	V	W	W	G	Z	R	V
G	G	V	W	V	G	V	V	V	W
V	G	G	G	G	W	V	V	G	V
W	M	W	G	V	V	G	V	G	V
V	G	V	W	V	M	V	G	G	W
G	V	V	G	G	G	G	V	G	G

Ready for a real challenge? Then try another one of my amazing Ken Ken puzzles. It's guaranteed to fry your brain, but only in a good way!

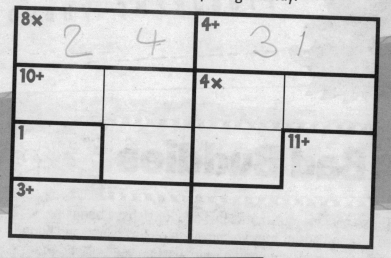

8x **2 4**		4+ **3 1**	
10+		4x	
1			11+
3+			

The aim is to fill each horizontal and vertical line of the box with the digits 1 - 4. The numbers must all appear once and once only in each line. In addition to this the numbers in each cell outlined in bold must add up to the small digit in the corner of the cell by the mathematical means stated. So 8 x means the two digits in that cell must add up to eight when multiplied, while 4 + means the two digits in that cell must make 4 when added together. Can you do it? Course you Ken!

NIFTY SHIFTY

There's no one in Monstro City shiftier than Sly Chance! Can you work out this puzzle by shifting each letter forward one place to find the name of the Dodgy Dealz proprietor's fave snack.

P T H B J R Z M C - V H B G D R

- - - - - - - - - - - - - - - -

Bad Buddies

Those mischievous mates Bug and Ratty have been up to no good again! They've shown up on Gift Island and buried someone under a mound of parcels. Can you tell who the unlucky victim might be?

. . . .

Moshling Maths

Who'd have thought you could have so much puzzling fun merely by totting up your Moshlings? Each critter in the Moshling Zoo has a serial number. Work out the sums to see what new Moshlings you can come up with.

A. #30 + #20 = #

B. #23 + #34 = #

C. #82 + #18 = #

Buster's Dream

Zzzzzz! Moshling maestro Buster's having a well-deserved rest - no doubt dreaming about his Moshi friends. Can you work out who he's dreaming about?

Write your answers here

1..................

2..................

3..................

Postcard in a Bottle

Ahoy land lubbers, Cap'n Buck here! Just hangin' with me hearties on my annual holiday! I've sent two postcards in a bottle back to Monstro City, but one of them has got smudged in the mail. Circle the five things that are missing on the second card. Arrrrr!

Mixed-Up Moshlings

Don't cha just want to thump those Glumps?! Now Strangeglove's loathsome lackeys have bounced into the Monstro City's archives and cut up all the photos. Which three Moshling pics have they mixed together here?

....
....
....

Tyra's Spa

Tyra Fangs is up to her hair extensions in paperwork today! She's trying to work out how many Rox she has spent on launching her new spa in Ooh La Lane. Can you help the gossip queen settle her accounts? Tyra needs to offset her launch costs against the money she's made in the first six months of trading.

SUPER TOUGH!

FIXTURES AND FITTINGS	ROX
WALLPAPER	100
CABINETS	750
MIRROR	89

DÉCOR	
CANDLES	260
VASES	156
RADIO	74
MAGAZINES	35

EQUIPMENT	
HAIRDRYER	40
SHOWER AND NOZZLE	52
TOWELS	103
SPONGES	77
BARS OF SOAP	400
MUD PACKS	470
SLOP AND GOO FACE PACKS	325
STINK EAU DE SOCKS	380

UTILITIES	
WATER BILL	1005
MONSTRO-WATTS BILL FROM EN-GEN	1670

MARKETING AND PUBLICITY	
LAUNCH PARTY	1400

ADD UP TYRA'S TOTAL EXPENDITURE HERE ... [   ]

TOTAL INCOME 12509

DELETE TYRA'S EXPENDITURE FROM
HER INCOME TO FIND OUT HER NET PROFIT.. [   ]

IF TYRA HAD TO PAY 10% OF HER NET
PROFIT IN MONSTRO CITY TAXES HOW
MUCH WOULD SHE OWE? .... [   ]

Slippy Fishy!

Fumbles are officially the clumsiest Moshlings in town! A visit to the Puzzle Palace always ends in tears - so many stairs! How many (not so) Acrobatic SeaStars are slipping and tumbling around the building today?

Write the number here.

SUPER TOUGH!

EYES SPY

He's the man in the know when it comes to Ice Scream, but can Giuseppe Gelato get to grips with this eyeball-based puzzle? And, more to the point, can you?

How many eyes have popped up on this page? Write your answer here.

They Call It
PUPPY LOVE

There sure are some cute, fluffy Moshlings around!
Can you guess who this little cuddlemuffin might be?
Read the rhyme, then write the Moshling's name and type in
the blank spaces.

**I'm pretty!
Would you like a smoochie?
Chuck my chin say 'coochy, coochy',
Pushy, swanky,
I'm so snooty,**

I'm _Gigi_ **, I'm the** _poochie poochie_ **!**

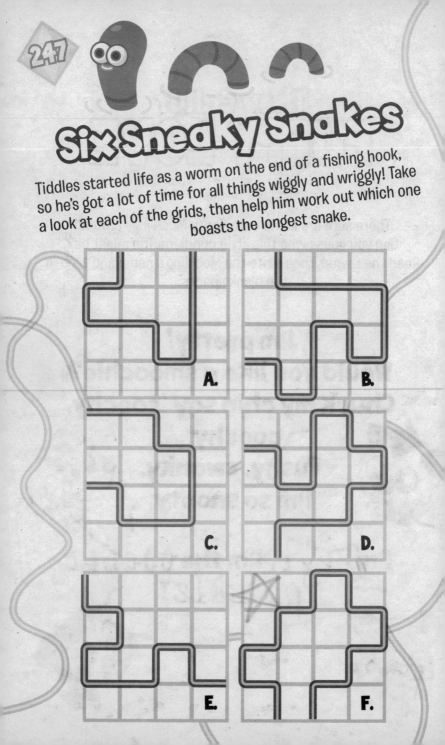

Six Sneaky Snakes

Tiddles started life as a worm on the end of a fishing hook, so he's got a lot of time for all things wiggly and wriggly! Take a look at each of the grids, then help him work out which one boasts the longest snake.

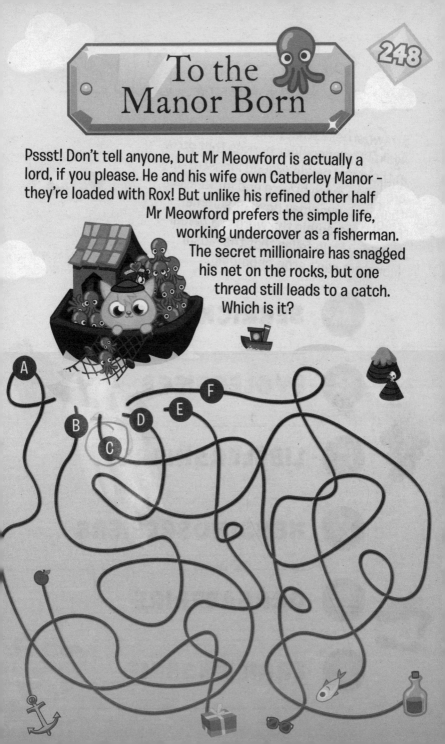

To the Manor Born

Pssst! Don't tell anyone, but Mr Meowford is actually a lord, if you please. He and his wife own Catberley Manor - they're loaded with Rox! But unlike his refined other half Mr Meowford prefers the simple life, working undercover as a fisherman. The secret millionaire has snagged his net on the rocks, but one thread still leads to a catch. Which is it?

Berry Nice

Strawberries? What? Blackberries? Come again? The succulent berries that grow in the countryside around Monstro City are much more bizarre and interesting than your everyday bowl of summer fruit! Unscramble the words to reveal the juicy little fellas that the Moshi Monsters can't stop chomping.

A SERRICKYUBE

_ _ _ _ _ _ _ _ _ _ _

B EVOLERBIERS

_ _ _ _ _ _ _ _ _ _ _

C LIBELERSHIRRS

_ _ _ _ _ _ _ _ _ _ _ _ _

D HENSINUSREBIERS

_ _ _ _ _ _ _ _ _ _ _ _ _ _ _

E ORRSABERIRE

_ _ _ _ _ _ _ _ _ _ _

F ERRILWSSBRIE

_ _ _ _ _ _ _ _ _ _ _ _

Blurp Spurt

Yeurk! Blurp's upset! The Batty Bubblefish has splurted multi-coloured gloop all over a poor, unsuspecting passer-by. Who's on the end of his monstrous deluge?

w u r l e y

_ _ _ _ _ _

Dipsy Downpour

They may look cute and smiley, but rub this Dinky Dreamcloud up the wrong way and you'll find yourself soaked to the skin within minutes! This Dipsy is enraged (perhaps a Glump has got her goat?) and she's letting loose a deluge.

SUPER TOUGH!

How many raindrops can you count?
Write your answer here.

Alphabet Soup

Can you answer all three letter questions in under thirty seconds? I scored a trio of right answers in twenty seconds this morning - beat that! Grab a pen and set your watch. Alphabetty, get setty, go!

1. Which letter appears more than once?

G ☐   M ☐

S ☐   W ☐

2. Which vowel is missing?

E ☐   I ☐

O ☐   U ☐

3. Which consonant is missing?

F ☐   G ☐

S ☐   K ☐

A	B	C	D	E
F	G	G	H	I
J	L	M	N	P
Q	R	S	T	U
V	W	X	Y	Z

Write your time in here

☐

I Love Lard!

Who's hiding behind this pile of cupcakes and candy canes? Give yourself a Monster pat on the back if you can name its species, too.

Need a clue? This critter is widely regarded as the couch potato of Moshlings — a cheery chubster with an obsession with confectionery.

Furi Knows Best

Elder Furi believes that only by studying that which is beneath our very noses, can we become all-knowing. We see the letters of the alphabet every day of our lives, but how closely do we really look at them?

Focus your mind, then check out the two rows of letters.

A E F H I K L M N T V W X Y Z
B C D G J O P Q R S U

What's the difference between them?

More Purplex-ing Riddles

Owls of Wiseness can't stop thinking up deep and difficult riddles! Here are some even more complex Purplex conundrums.

SUPER TOUGH!

Why can it be said that Sunday is the strongest day of the week?

....

What can go up a chimney down but can't go down a chimney up?

....

Many have heard it, but no one has seen it and it will not speak until spoken to. What is it?

....

When I lead a group, its strength stays the same, but if I follow it, the group's strength increases ten times! I am as simple as a circle, but amount to nothing. What am I?

....

Mudpack Moshlings

Mwah! Mwah! Absolutely divine to meet you dahling! These four fa-a-a-bulous Moshlings have never done a proper day's work in their lives. The gorgeous group shares a common appreciation of anything pretty, sparkly and fun. Here they're having an all-over mud pack at Tyra's Spa. Can you guess their diva identities and write down their types and categories too?

_ _ _ _ _ _
....
....

_ _ _ _
_ _ _ _ _ _
....
....

_ _ _ _ _
....
....

_ _ _ _
....
....

MANIC MATCH

You're going to have to be sharper than IGGY's spikes to tackle this pattern puzzle! Look closely at the squares below, then check out the ticker tape printouts below. Which of the four samples is an accurate and absolute representation of each line?

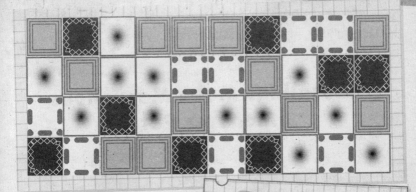

1.
```
A A C A A B D A B A
A B C A A A B D D A
C A C B C D D A B B
A B C A A B B D D B
```

3.
```
A B C A A A B D D A
C A C C D D A C B B
D C B C A C C A C A
B D A A B D B C D C
```

2.
```
C A C C D D A C B B
C B C A D D D A B A
C A C D B A A C B B
D A C D B A C D B A
```

4.
```
B D A B B D B C C D
C D A B B D B C D C
C D A A B D B C D C
B D A A B D B C D C
```

5.
```
NONE OF THE
ABOVE
```

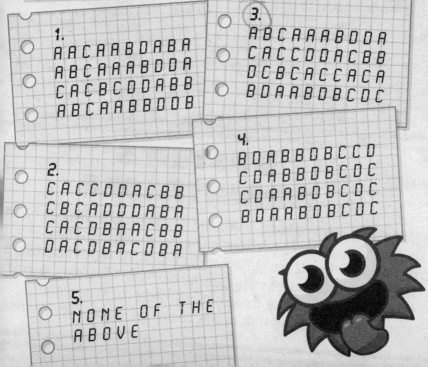

Word Up!

258

Zack Binspin is running an über-fan competition. The winner may or may not get tickets to his next tour! It all depends whether he decides to cancel!

Anyhoo, here's the challenge he's set you. How many different phrases can you create using the letters in the following sentence?

Moshlings Make Marvellous Monster Pets

....
....
....
....
....

BUSTER'S BRAINTEASER

259

Buster was captured by a hostile tribe of Moshlings. The chief told Buster he could make one statement that would determine what happened to him. If the statement was false, he would be boiled in water. If the statement were true, he would be fried in oil. Buster Bumblechops didn't like these options, so he came up with a statement that got him out of this seemingly impossible situation

She should be so lucky, lucky, lucky, lucky . . . oh wait, she already is! Tingaling is a new Moshling in town - bumping into her could be the best thing that ever happens to you. Why is this mystic Moshling always welcomed with open arms? Shift the letters of the alphabet forward by one to unscramble Tingaling's type.

JHSSDM NE FNNC ENQSTMD

_ _ _ _ _ _   _ _   _ _ _ _ _

_ _ _ _ _ _ _

Don't forget to SHIFT before you scribble! Remember B = C, C = D and so on . . .

What is the one statement he could have made to save his bacon?

....

....

....

....

PETIT PORT QUIZ

If you go down to The Port today, you're in for a big surprise! Instead of having a browse in Babs' Boutique or setting sail for Gift Island, the Moshis have devised a true or false quiz to keep themselves entertained! Study this view of The Port, and then tick the correct boxes.

1. Mr Meowford is crewing his ship alone.
☐ True ☐ False

2. Dr. Strangeglove is standing next to Kissy.
☐ True ☐ False

3. IGGY is getting a lift in Percy's beak.
☐ True ☐ False

4. Cap'n Buck is flying a 'jolly roger' skull and crossbones flag.
☐ True ☐ False

5. There are eight boats in the water.
☐ True ☐ False

6. Burnie is setting fire to Percy.
☐ True ☐ False

7. Beau Squiddly has caught Coolio on the end of his line.
☐ True ☐ False

8. Lefty is looking through a telescope.
☐ True ☐ False

RANSOM!

Baddie Dr. Strangeglove has kidnapped the Gatekeeper - now no one is keeping watch over Super Moshi HQ! The villain's ransom note has got ripped and burned during the scuffle outside the volcano. Can you piece it together to find out Strangeglove's twisted terms? Draw a line from each scrap of paper to its place on the opposite page and then write the message above.

Ng a d...
StrangeGL
RaTORy!

Dr S
LaBO

be a...

per Mos
you DeL

fRAid. BE vEr...
...have

we h...
Keeper. V
to PoUN

We arE
ce On

y
vOuR

SHis
iVER

poised
tHE Su
unless
A Mosl

afraID

gaTe
ove's

ly To

Be ___ ___, ___ ___ ___, ___ ___ ___
___ ___ ___ ___ ___ ___ ___ ___, ___ ___
___ ___ ___ ___ ___ ___ ___ ___
___ ___ ___ ___ ___ ___ ___ ___ ___ ___
___ ___ ___ ___ ___ ___ ___ ___ ___, ___
___ ___ ___ ___!

SCARE SQUARES

DIAVLO'S A FANGTASTICALLY DEVILISH
LITTLE SO-AND-SO! THIS SMOKIN' SET OF
SCARE SQUARES HAS BEEN DESIGNED TO
TEST ALL HOTHEADS TO THE LIMIT.
TAKE A LOOK AT THE JUMBLED SHAPES
AND THEN TOT UP THE TOTAL.

SUPER
TOUGH!

Shape Shake

Study the contents of this frame, taking care to observe every detail. Now grab a pen and work your way through the questions. Can you nail them all in less than half a minute?

1. How many squares are there in total?

....

2. What black shape isn't touching any diamonds?

....

3. Are there more triangles or circles?

....

4. Which shape does not appear in black?

....

Sillyham Snap

The *Daily Growl* is about to go to press with the first official photo of His Royal MonSTARness Prince Sillyham and his long-term lady love Kate Giggleton, but some joker (possibly a Chop Chop) has doctored the picture. Check it against the original and circle six things that have been changed.

The Daily Growl

Calling all word whizzes, letter loons and spelling smarty-pants!
My lab computer has generated a timed test that is bound to
have you begging for a dictionary. Set your stopwatch to sixty
seconds, then give these teasers a try.

Which of the words below is hidden in the grid?

POD ☐   NOD ☐

DIP ☐   NOT ☐

Which of the words below is not in the grid?

INN ☐   ANT ☐

PET ☐   DOG ☐

Pick seven letters from the grid,
then use them to create a brand
new word. Write it here.

_ _ _ _ _ _ _

Rockin' Rooms

Is your room a shrine to minimalism or as cluttered as a crowd of Cutie Pies? Every Monster knows that their crib is the ultimate style statement! Use this quick quiz to gen up on the latest trends in Moshi interiors.

1. Which of these chairs is not a genuine Moshi product?

A. Breakfast Bayou Sausage Sofa ☐   **B.** Barf-alona Chair ☐

C. Chair of the Future ☐   **D.** The Drool Stool ☐

2. How much should you expect to pay for a Fried Egg Rug?

A. 114 Rox ☐   **B.** 45 Rox ☐

C. 150 Rox ☐   **C.** 99 Rox ☐

3. Which bowl-dwelling aquatic creature is a popular pet in many Monster homes?

A. A tadpole ☐   **B.** A mudsucking Gwindle ☐

C. A seahorse ☐   **C.** A mini-shark ☐

4. Which of these is not a bona fide Cuddly Human?

A. Cuddly Cowboy ☐   B. Cuddly Fisherman ☐

C. Cuddly Plumber ☐   D. Cuddly Teacher ☐

5. One of these Wallscrawl letters from Babs' Boutique costs more than the three others. Which is it?

A. Q ☐   B. L ☐

C. A ☐   D. T ☐

6. Which personality carries out 'What's Hot Right Now' tours around Monstro City in her guise as a home fashion expert?

A. Babs ☐   B. Tyra Fangs ☐

C. Ms Snoots ☐   D. Ruby Scribblez ☐

Quick Triv:
Which Moshling would absolutely lov
to be kept in a clutter-free monster
home? _ _ _ _ _ _

Tricky Tongue Twister

If he wasn't trapped in a head spin next to his mega-amped boom box, Max Volume would be awesome at these tongue twisters. As he's tied up right now, why don't you have a go? Try rattling through each phrase six times over without coming unstuck.

Strangeglove strategically stalks Snookums.

Wonderful Worldies wave wildly when woken.

Purdy the Tubby Huggishi is greedy, catty and lardy.

Fabulous, furry Furis face friendly, fluffy flumps.

Never, never, never nick a naughty Ninja's noodles.

EGG-STREMELY MESSY

Did you know that Gross-ery guru Snozzle Wobbleson started out as a lowly stock monster? Here he is, pictured on his first day at the store, just after dropping a whole crate of eggs. Count how many eggs Snozzle dropped.

Write your answer here.

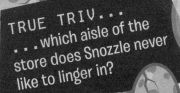

TRUE TRIV...
...which aisle of the store does Snozzle never like to linger in?

Moshling Homework

Pete and Lila are out picnicking – again! Lila is talking Pete through her singing ambitions – again! Instead of munching on Quenut Butter Sandwiches, the pair should really be doing their homework. Can you give them a hand with their geography? This week they're studying Earth.

1. How much of planet Earth is covered by water?

 Around 65%   Around 70%

 Around 40%   Around 80%

2. How many humans have walked on the moon?

 2   22

 12   32

3. Who invented the Internet?

 Tim Berners-Lee   Charles Babbage

 Bill Gates   Hewlett Packard

4. What is a rhinoceros' horn made of?

- Muscle
- Bone
- Skin
- Keratin

5. What is the capital of Belgium?

- Bruges
- Brussels
- Ghent
- Antwerp

6. Which planet was recently downgraded and re-classified as a star?

- Saturn
- Pluto
- Jupiter
- Neptune

SUPER TOUGH!

ShiShi Sudoku

Aah-choo! These cute Beasties lurve watching Monstrovision, but it makes their noses irresistibly tickly. Sneezing Pandas have to make sure that they're permanently armed with tissues and magical eye-drops!

Have a crack at this ShiShi Sudoku puzzle. Each of the pictures must only appear once on each horizontal and vertical line, and each 4 x 4 box.

Crazy Quilt

It's me again, puzzlers, the undisputed quilting queen of Monstro City! Like my latest designs? Only one of these stitched squares is truly unique. Which is it?

A

B

C

D

E

F

G

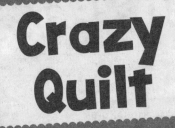
H

I

Ken Ken Tickles

He might be a construction Roarker, but Ken Tickles loves a mental challenge! His third eye comes in extra handy when checking these number grids. Are you ready to help him solve this Ken Ken puzzle?

6+	3+	**1**	3
	3-	7+	3+
3			
4+		2-	

Fill each horizontal and vertical line of the box with the digits 1 to 4. Each number must appear once only in each line. The numbers in each cage must add up to the small digit in the corner of the cell by the mathematical means stated. So 8 x means the two digits in that cell must add up to eight when multiplied, while 4 + means the two digits in that cell must make 4 when added together.

Phoney Pony

This page was supposed to feature two fangtablous Pony Moshlings, but their pictures have been well and truly jigsawed! Study the stacked shapes, then name the horsey pair.

1. ....

2. ....

Did you notice that a third, phoney pony has muscled in, too? Write down the imposter's name and species.

3. ....

Growl Style

He's the most famous talent scout in Monstro City and h
wears his trousers really, really high! What else do you kı
about the music industry legend that is Simon Growl?

How many years in succession has Simon
been voted the meanest judge at the
Underground Disco?

....

Who are the other two judges on the panel?

....

How can you tell how Simon is feeling, without
even speaking to him?

....

What is the mogul's mansion made out of?

....

How can visitors get from the house to the pool?

....

What other feature dominates Simon's garden?

....

Snappy Sequences

Cheese is always the answer when Gingersnap's part of the equation, but you may have to think on if you want to ace this number sequence puzzle – 'Brie' or 'Cheddar' ain't gonna score you many points! Put the missing numbers back into these sequences. When you've cracked each one, write down the rule behind each pattern.

A. 1   3   6   _   15   21   _   _

....

B. 200   175   150   _   100   _   _

....

C. 1   2   4   8   16   _   64   _

....

D. 1   1   2   3   5   _   13   _

....

E. 6000   3000   _   750   325

....

SUPER TOUGH!

H2OH!!!

Here's one to test your tentacles.
Who is this little sea shanty describing?

I'm the H2O queen
You may well have seen
me, I bob in the Port night and day.

I spout and I spritz,
A fine and fresh mist,
Which beats bath and shower, they say.

My name is ....

Line Dance

These parallel lines are positively loopy!
Can you count them all up before they
take over the page? Write the
total number of separate lines
in the box.

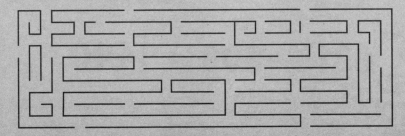

NO CALCULATORS, PLEASE! LET YOUR BRAIN TAKE THE STRAIN.

MATHS MASH

Ready to mash it up, Moshi fans? Pick up a pen and get number crunching! Fill the missing digits and symbols into each of the complex calculations below.

96 ÷ _ = 32

SUPER TOUGH!

73 − _ = 48

45 × 7 = _ _ _

422 ÷ _ = 105.5

631 _ 809 = 1440

What a Poppet!

They're the most huggalicious Moshis around, but did you know that there's more to these cute critters than pretty paws and big blue eyes? Find a pen and then put your Poppet know-how to the test.

1. What language do Poppets speak?

A. Monsterish ☐ B. Poppetish ☐ C. Poppetan ☐ D. Poppsish ☐

2. What do Poppets do if you get answers incorrect on the Daily Challenge?

A. Laugh ☐ B. Moonwalk ☐ C. Cry ☐ D. Sulk ☐

3. What is Poppet's original, non-customised colour?

A. Orange ☐ B. Pink ☐ C. Purple ☐ D. Red ☐

4. What do Poppets do with their hands if they're hungry or sick?

A. Put them on their tummy ☐ B. Wave them in the air ☐
C. Fold them in front of them ☐ D. Wring them ☐

5. What is the only item of clothing worn by a Poppet when you first meet it?

A. A hat ☐ B. A pair of boots ☐
C. A neck tie ☐ D. A bow tie ☐

6. Which of these words does not describe a Poppet?

A. Bashful ☐ B. Sweet ☐
C. Timid ☐ D. Irritable ☐

7. What do Poppets love to do?

A. Boogie ☐ B. Swim ☐
C. Wrestle ☐ D. Knit ☐

8. What might a Poppet do if you abandon or annoy them?

A. Curl up in a ball ☐ B. Throw themselves into Potion Ocean ☐
C. Go shopping ☐ D. Scream loudly ☐

Waldo's Wacky Word Box

Now then . . . you may have thought you had Waldo's Wacky Word Boxes sussed. Think again! This time the letter square has four clues to solve. In this mini-crossword, the answer to each clue is filled in across and down the grid.

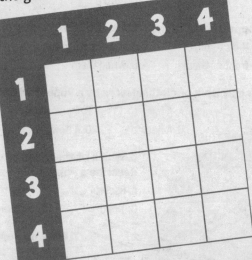

CLUES

1. Device used to grind salt and pepper.
2. An inventive thought.
3. You need one to walk a dog.
4. Female version of a gentleman.

Remember to write each answer across as well as down!

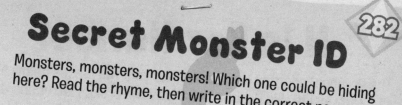

Secret Monster ID

Monsters, monsters, monsters! Which one could be hiding here? Read the rhyme, then write in the correct name.

I'm heart-shaped and gorgeous,
a bit of a gem,
I'm the only Moshi with a star-tipped stem.
Not every monster in town is this pretty,
I grace every place when I roam Monstro City.

••

Shuffle Kerfuffle

Avril LeScream is tired of touring with the Moshi MonStars and is looking for a hip new pad in Monstro City to relax in. Shuffle the letters to discover the style of pad that she's after.

R	Y	S	C	K	P	E	A	R	S

H is For Hansel

The Psycho Gingerboy has a puzzle for you! The pieces below all fit neatly inside this H, but how? Study the broken letter shards, then draw each one in place on the big letter. Can you rebuild the H in under two minutes? Every piece has to be used and has to fit exactly.

Cutie Chase

Eek! Something's trying to eat this Cutie Pie! The poor Wheelie YumYum needs to lay her hands on an exit strategy, fast! Help the Moshling find the best way through the canyon, into the safety of Candy Cane Caves.

A.

B.

C.

D.

E.

Crazy Creature

You may have seen this critter hustling on the streets of Monstro City – he covers the rent on his Sludgetown Apartment by performing tricks. It's just a shame he can't resist blowing any cash he does earn on his fave snack – Pop Rox.

Cross out all the letters that appear more than once in this grid. Now rearrange the ones that are left over to reveal the mystery Moshi name.

C	G	A	G	M	G	O	C	H	A
F	D	G	U	I	Z	D	F	I	F
H	J	U	J	E	C	W	A	Q	U
I	R	M	H	Z	T	D	U	U	K
U	I	U	C	S	D	M	G	W	M
A	L	F	U	H	J	W	F	I	C
A	D	J	N	I	D	A	L	H	C
T	H	G	M	Z	J	F	L	B	I
I	W	A	T	F	C	D	G	T	U
Q	C	Z	H	T	C	J	H	W	G

The crazy creature is ....

HUM PLUM, YOU'RE ON MY TUM!

Hum Plum was on the hunt for food for her children, when she wandered onto someone's tummy. Could be awkward! Who exactly is she climbing up?

BIG clue: He can often be seen stationed on Main Street, sleeping on the job!

Honey Hunt

How about a wordsearch where you actually learn stuff at the same time? This page is packed full of info about Funny Bunnies. Test your knowledge and your searching skills by looking up all of the words on the letter grid. Stay Fluffy and focussed - each one could be running in any direction.

☐	BUNNY	Honeys are Funny ones
☐	CARROT CAKE	They just love the stuff
☐	CHATTY	Honeys can't stop yacking
☐	FASHIONISTA	What every one of these Fluffies aims to become
☐	FLOPPY EAR	Experts think this is caused by listening to silly ringtones
☐	FUR	Honeys use straighteners on theirs to get their cute look
☐	CLOTHES	Funny Bunnies can't own enough of them
☐	HUTCHES	No earthy burrows for these critters
☐	IRONING	Honeys do this to flowers, especially Naffodils
☐	PAWBERRY	The name of the fields where most Honeys dwell
☐	SILLY	The kind of jokes that Funny Bunnies love to snigger at

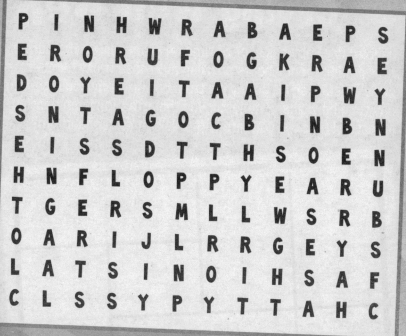

Crying Ken Ken

Jailbird Cry Baby has a lot of time on his hands, so the purple first grader spends hours puzzling out these tricky number grids. Prison can be boring it's true, but Cry Baby could get out any time he wishes - he just loves the attention from passing Monsters! How will you fare with this Ken Ken conundrum?

7+	4+	3+	
		2	7+
3+	6+		
	7+		1

Fill each horizontal and vertical line of the box with the digits 1 to 4. They must all appear once and once only in each line. Don't forget that the numbers in each cage must add up to the small digit in the corner of the cell by the mathematical means stated.

FURI FACTS

You'll need to scribble Furi-ously to get the answers to these questions! Don't get down in the dumps, Moshi Masters are sure to ace a perfect six. How much do you know about these grouchy, slouchy hairballs?

1. What language do Furis speak?
A. Monsterish   B. Furnese
C. Furian   D. Furic

2. What is Furi's favourite food?
A. Goo   B. Gunk
C. Fried Hairballs   D. Slop

3. What's the best thing that an owner can do for their Furi?
A. Wash them   B. Tickle them
C. Take them to the   D. Leave them alone
   Underground Disco

4. Name one of the major drawbacks of owning a Furi.
A. They sleep all the time   B. They get bored easily
C. They disappear from   D. They cry if their fur gets wet
   their room

5. What mythical creature does Furi most resemble?
A. Bandersnatch   B. Hobbit
C. Big Foot   D. Godzilla

6. Which of these words does not describe a Furi?
A. Loving   B. Hairy
C. Grouchy   D. Mean

SUPER TOUGH!

PILFERER'S PRICE MATCH

Those trouble-making Glumps have barged their way into Luvli Looks! Strangelove's heartless minions have pinched a stack of garments and ripped off the price tags. Can you match each item with the right tag so the poor Luvli storeowner can work out how much each Glump owes?

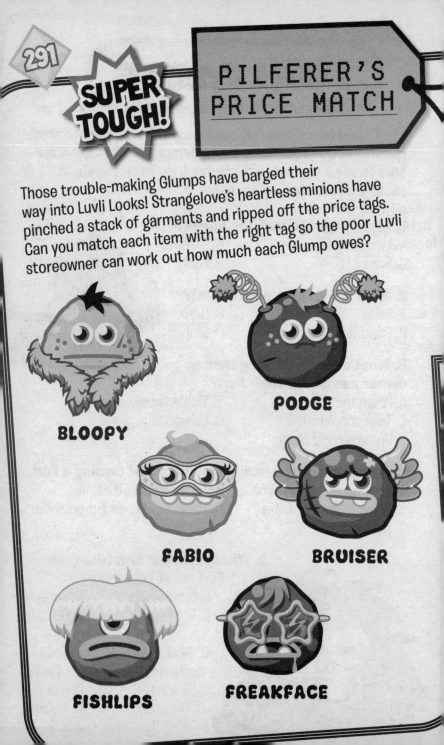

BLOOPY

PODGE

FABIO

BRUISER

FISHLIPS

FREAKFACE

Bling out your wings with this shiny upgrade.

144 Rox

How lush. Made from fur that dropped off a Furi.

70 Rox

Do blondes really have more fun? Wig up and work it out!

60 Rox

Guaranteed to make everything look technicolour fantastic!

30 Rox

The ultimate MonSTAR accessory!!

34 Rox

77 Rox

Because even Glumps have a sense of humour.

292

Moshi Manners

Who ate all the pies? When it's time to chow down, Moshis don't wait to be invited! This trio of voracious monsters are having a scoff-fest on sticky, icky snacks from the Gross-ery Store. Take a look at the mess, then hazard a guess at what they've been eating.

BLOCK PARTY

This Zommer was so busy rocking out on the way to a Moshi MonStars gig, he lost his way. Can you help him get to the venue in time?

Find Zommer, then move him two blocks west, four blocks north, three blocks south, three blocks east and then one last block south. Where does he end up? Draw a circle around the letter marking his destination.

F		D		F			A	
G	A	A	D	G			F
E	F	C	B	E	D	C	
A	G	D	B	A	D	B	B
C	D	E		D	B		A
A	F	C	B	C	E		
C	B	A	F	A		B	
G	B		B	F		G

Stanley's Show Tunes

Songful Seahorses love belting out show tunes! What are Stanley's all time faves? Use the key below to crack the code, then write the titles beneath them. Feel free to whistle while you work!

1. ☐≡✗ ≡⊣Иϡ☐✿ ≡⊣Иⅰϡ ☐ИⅠ✗ ☐И⊣∷✗ ∷⊣☐≡ ☐≡✗ ϡ◉<◉☐ ◉✚ ⋏◉◼≡Иϡ

___ _____ ____ ____ ___ ___
____ ___ _____ __ _____

2. ⊣☐ ϡ ✿ ≡✿ИⅠ И◉⦂Ⅰ: И⊣✚✗

__'_ _ ____ ___ ____

3. ϡ≡⊣ϡ≡⊣ ϡ≡⊣ϡ≡⊣ •ǀ•✿◆✳ •ǀ•✿◆✳

_____ _____ ____ ____

4. ⊥<ϡ☐ ✿ ϡЛ◉◉◉◆✚<И ◉✚ ✳И◉◉∩

____ _ _____ __ _____

5. ▽✿◆)◉< ✚✗∷И ☐≡✗ И<⦂И⊣ ☐◉◆⊣✳≡☐

___ ___ ____ ___ ____
_____?

6. ◉⦂∷Л ☐≡✗ Л◉) ✳ •ǀ•⊣⊣ Л✿⊣◆•ǀ•◉✗

____ ___ ___ ___. ___ _____

Key

A = ✿	N = ◆
B = •ǀ•	O = ◉
C = ▽	P = ∩
D = ◼	Q = Ω
E = ✗	R = Л
F = ✚	S = Ϡ
G = ✳	T = ☐
H = ≡	U = <
I = ⊣	V = ⋮
J = ⊥	W = ✗
K = ✖	X = ∷
L = И	Y =)
M = ⋏	Z = Ø

Bubble Trouble

Think you can catch a Batty Bubblefish by watching its air bubbles rising to the surface? You're more likely to glimpse one with its head out of the water, blowing a raspberry! Study this grid, then give these bubbly questions a try.

1. Which bubble appears most often? ....

SUPER TOUGH!

2. Which bubbles only pop up in pairs? ....

3. How many black bubbles are there? ....

4. How many bubbles are not touching a white bubble? ....

5. Which type of bubble doesn't feature on the top row? ....

FLAG FRENZY

Dr. Strangeglove can be maddening at times! Now Monstro City's naughty nemesis has singlehandedly sucked all of the colour out of these country flags. Luckily their designs are distinctive and unique, even in black and white.

Study the flags, then use the country list to identify each one.

1.....................

2.....................

3.....................

4.....................

5.....................

UNITED KINGDOM
WALES
ISRAEL
SOUTH AFRICA
USA

297

chock-a-block

Beau Squiddly is expecting a bumper haul today! The canny angler has invested in a load of boxes to house all the fish he's going to land. Exactly how many boxes has Beau brought?

SUPER TOUGH!

Write your answer in here.

ART'S ART

298

Art Lee's done some of his amazing graffiti work on this wall. This time he's created a spray-can portrait of a Moshi Monster. Join up the dots to reveal who Art has drawn.

Fact or Fib?

Real Moshi fanatics should breeze through this true or false quiz. Take the test and then check your answers at the back of the book. Are you a Silly Snuffler or an Owl of Wiseness?

1. Sneezing Pandas love channel hopping.

☐ Fact
☐ Fib

2. Babs' Boutique is on Main Street.

☐ Fact
☐ Fib

3. The Googenheim Gallery is where you can view monster owners' art.

☐ Fact
☐ Fib

4. Dragon Berries are a seed used to catch Moshlings.

☐ Fact
☐ Fib

5. Six striped candy canes can be spotted outside the Candy Cane Caves.

☐ Fact
☐ Fib

6. Dr. Strangeglove's henchmen are known as Flumps.

☐ Fact
☐ Fib

7. Katsumas have pointed, arrow-shaped tails.

☐ Fact
☐ Fib

8. An ominous purple airship frequently glides over Monstro City.

☐ Fact
☐ Fib

9. Roland Jones is obsessed with drinking Toad Soda.

☐ Fact
☐ Fib

10. A Squidge is a loveable Puppy.

☐ Fact
☐ Fib

How did you do?

LESS THAN 5

Sorree! You are almost certainly a Silly Snuffler.

MORE THAN 5

Hats off to your mighty Moshiness, you are a true Owl of Wiseness.

300 EYES SPY

Hello Moshi maniacs, I'm checking in again with another Eyes Spy puzzle! You're probably rolling your eyes skyward by now, but I can't get enough of these tricky teasers!

Carefully tot up the eyeballs. Write the total in this box.

More Batty Boxes

This Batty Bubblefish is even more confused by this series of puzzles. It's up to you to think outside the box and get each one cracked! Remember - all you gotta do is say what you see.

1.
LION
LION
LION
LION

AUTUMN
IN THE
USA

2.
idnilb

3.
WHETHER
Cast Cast
Cast Cast

4.
HEAD
HEEL HEEL

5.
Oh o oh o oh o oh o
O oh o oh o oh o oh
Oh o oh DOM o oh o
O oh o oh o oh o oh
Oh o oh o oh o oh o

6.
LOG

Waldo's Wacky Word Box

OMG . . . it's another Tabby Nerdicat brainbuster! Remember, Waldo's word puzzles work just like mini-crosswords, except the answer to each clue is filled in across and down the grid at the same time. Got it? Good!

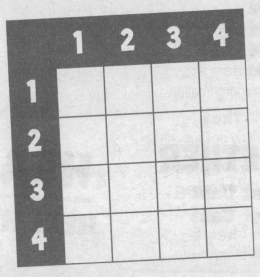

	1	**2**	**3**	**4**
1				
2				
3				
4				

CLUES

1. Congealed blood.
2. When a horse can't walk.
3. Leave out.
4. French word for 'head'.

Remember to write each answer across as well as down!

Gurgle Choosums

What do you know about this little Dino? The possibilities are very similar and all seem plausible – but some are fact and some are fake, fake, FAKE! The decision is up to you – choosums or lose-ums.

1. Are Gurgles ...
Rare or Ultra Rare?

2. Do they live in ...
The Crazy Canyon or
Cupcake Canyon?

3. Do they most enjoy eating ...
Toasted Marshmallows or Roasted Barfmallows?

4. Are they ...
camera shy or fame hungry?

5. Are Gurgles also known as Performing ...
Flappasauruses or Actosauruses?

6. Are they best described as ...
sensitive or insensitive?

7. Is their Moshling number ...
83 or 38?

8. Do they most dislike ...
bad audiences and soggy matches or bad reviews and magic tricks?

NIFTY SHIFTY

Admit it, monster owner! When it comes to this item in your Moshi home, bigger and bushier is most definitely better. Can you guess what I'm talking about? Shift the alphabet back four places to find out.

JVMIRHW XVII

_ _ _ _ _ _ _   _ _ _ _

Don't forget to SHIFT before you scribble! Remember E = A, F = B, G = C and so on...

Vowel Howl

As Moshlings go, General Fuzuki's got more vowels in his moniker than most! Here's an extreme Vowel Howel to put your puzzle prowess to the test.

Which of these six letter words has all of its vowels in the same position as the word at the top? Give yourself no more than ten seconds to tick the right box.

NINJAS

ALIGNS ☐
UNREST ☐
PLANET ☐
PERMIT ☐

Buster's Ranch

Welcome to Buster's Ranch. The place is always chocker with Moshi wildlife, but Señor Bumblechops does have a particular penchant for cows - they're better than lawnmowers, don'tcha know! How many are currently grazing outside Buster's pad?

Write your answer here.

HOT HEAD

What's not to like about Diavlo? Try and correctly answer all eight questions about these sizzly-fizzly lava heads. Don't blow your top if you can't!

1. What language does Diavlo speak?

A. DIAVLORN ☐   B. DIAVLIAN ☐

C. DIAVLISH ☐   D. MONSTERISH ☐

2. What do Diavlos have in their heads?

A. LAVA ☐   B. POPCORN ☐

C. STRAWBERRY JAM ☐   D. FIZZY POP ☐

3. Which of these words best describes Diavlo?

A. SLEEPY ☐   B. BORING ☐

C. QUIET ☐   D. MISCHIEVIOUS ☐

4. What happens when Diavlo gets angry?

A. IT SHOOTS LAVA FROM ITS HEAD ☐   B. ITS TAIL SPINS AROUND ☐

C. IT GOES UP IN FLAMES ☐   D. IT BREATHES FIRE ☐

5. What do Diavlo's wings enable it to do?

A. GET ON WITH BIRDIES ☐   B. DO BRILLIANT DANCE MOVES ☐

C. TICKLE THEMSELVES ☐   D. FLY ☐

6. Which of these words does not describe a Diavlo?

A. SHY ☐   B. FIERY ☐

C. CONFIDENT ☐   D. CUTE ☐

7. What are Diavlo's original colours?

A. BLACK AND RED ☐   B. BLACK AND PURPLE ☐

C. RED AND GREEN ☐   D. RED AND YELLOW ☐

8. What do Diavlos wear on their feet?

A. ROLLERSKATES ☐   B. SLIPPERS ☐

C. TRAINERS ☐   D. HIGH HEELS ☐

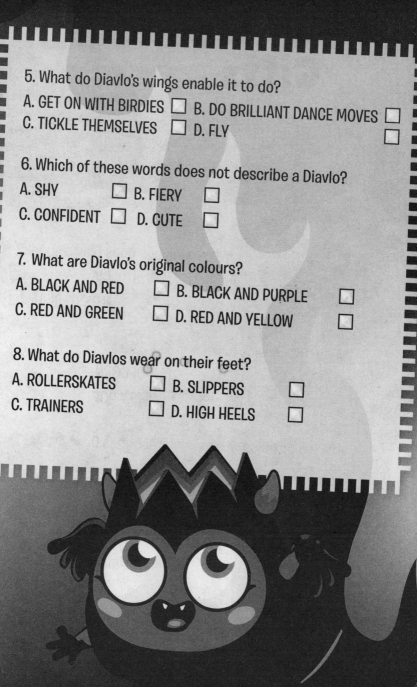

Shifted Gifts

Gift Island is groaning with presents today, and it's not even Twistmas! Some strange Moshi madness has split this scene into five higgledy-piggledy slices. Can you put it back together again?

A

B

C

Write the correct sequence here.

_ _ _ _ _

Mixed-up Moshlings

Which three yummy friends are hiding here?
Write your answers below.

1. ....

2. ....

3. ....

All done? Wowsers!
You're a Moshlingologist in the making!

Line Dance

Uh-oh! There's a sale on at Poppet's Closet - just look at the queue. While you and your Monster wait your turn, see if you can work out exactly how many lines are racked up across this page.

How many separate ones can you pick out?

SECRET WORD

What d'ya think that Liberty has in her hand 24/7? Yep, you guessed it – it's the latest copy of Tamara Tesla's secret word puzzles – Worldies go crazy for these wordy grids! You've got sixty seconds to beat the Happy Statue at her own game. Can you do it?

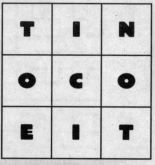

T	I	N
O	C	O
E	I	T

Which of the following words is not contained in the grid?

NOT ☐   TIN ☐

TOE ☐   PIN ☐

Which of the words below features backwards in the grid?

PEN ☐   SON ☐

TIE ☐   COO ☐

Use the letters from the grid to make at least two new four letter words. Write them below.

_ _ _ _   _ _ _ _

_ _ _ _   _ _ _ _

After spotting Liberty's word puzzle, Mini Ben wants to get in on the act! He's set you some extreme time-based puzzles. Answer with care: these brainbusters just get trickier and trickier . . .

SUPER TOUGH!

What time is the clock above saying now?

A. 1.55 ☐ B. 1.42 ☐

C. 2.12 ☐ D. 1.22 ☐

If the hour hand of a clock moves 1/60th of a degree every minute, how many degrees will it move in an hour?

....

How many hands are there on the clock on London's Big Ben?

....

How many times do the hands of a clock overlap in twenty-four hours?

....

If it were two hours later, it would be half as long until midnight as it would be if it were an hour later. What time is it now?

....

How many degrees are there between the big and little clock hands when the time says 3.15 pm?

....

Crazy Quilt

Furi's fingers are so chubby they'd never be able to thread a needle, so this is the closest it can get to embroidery. Can you see which of the squares below has a tiny flaw in it? Furi can, but he's too grumpy to tell, so you'll have to work it out for yourself!

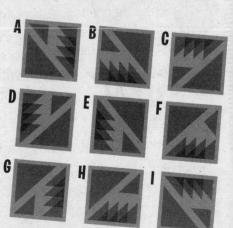

A B C
D E F
G H I

Funny Bunnies

These adorable white Fluffies seem to multiply faster than you can say 'happy hopscotch'! Goodness knows what's been happening to these Honeys in Pawberry Fields. Count up the Funny Bunnies hopping across the page.

There are .... Funny Bunnies.

How many would there be if they each

brought a friend? ....

How many more would there be if they each

had two friends? ....

Super Scramble

Be confused, be very confused! This puzzle is chock full of overlapping letters. Carefully pick your way through the alphabet shapes, jotting down every letter that you recognise. Now rearrange each set to reveal a fistful of monstrous new names.

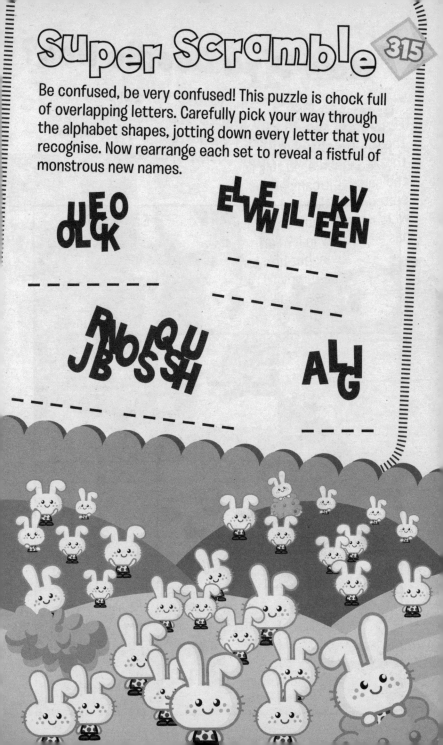

How D'ya Doodle Doo?

Greetings Moshi fans, Roary Scrawl at your service! Would you like to step into my study? It's the place where I've scribbled some of my greatest ever *Daily Growl* articles!

If you want to explore my writing room, you'll need to earn the privilege. Copy each square from the grid below into the matching letter square on the facing page. Join 'em all together and you'll have penned your own work of art in no time at all.

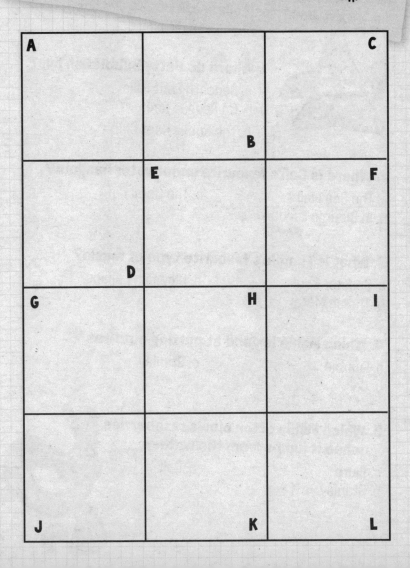

FISHTORY TEST

If you've never studied Fishtory, you might be worried about sitting a test on the subject. Don't panic, you already know the most important element linking these Moshlings. Here's a clue - it's wet and blue! Let's see what else you know . . .

1. Where do Batty Bubblefish live?
a. Beneath Fruit Falls
b. On Reggae Reef
c. The Rocky Reef Club

2. Where is Cali's favourite underwater hangout?
a. The Sea Mall
b. In Bleurgh Lagoon
c. The Coral Cafe

3. What is Fumble's favourite type of music?
a. Seastar Soul
b. Thrash Metal
c. Blowfish Ballads

4. Which Fishie is good at putting out fires?
a. Fumble
b. Cali
c. Stanley

5. Which Fishie often blows raspberries when it jumps from the water?
a. Blurp
b. Stanley
c. Cali

6. What happens to Cali's headband heart when she senses romance?

a. It grows to three times the size
b. It flashes
c. It delivers a love note

7. To catch a Blurp, what do you need to plant?

a. Moon Orchid (any), Love Berries (any), Love Berries (pink)
b. Moon Orchid (Blue), Dragon Fruit (any), Love Berries (any)
c. Love Berries (pink), Magic Beans (any), Star Blossom (any)

8. Which group of Fishies is ultra rare?

a. Songful Seahorses
b. Batty Bubblefish and Valley Mermaids
c. None of the above

9. How is Fumble's personality described?

a. Scatty, crochety, bewildered
b. Gnarly, fearless, full of beans
c. Flamboyant, tactless, noisy

10. Which Fishie enjoys a dip in the bath as much as a swim in the sea?

a. Cali
b. Stanley
c. Fumble

Shape Shake

This puzzle's the shape of things to come, guys! Set your stopwatch, Rock Clock or eye-Phone to thirty seconds, then rocket through the quiz questions below.

1. What is the least common shape on the board?

....

2. How many squares are there in total?

....

3. Which shape is not touching any shade of pentagon?

....

4. How many shapes are black?

....

Bats In The Belfry

319

Wing, Fang, Screech and Sonar used to live in Ecto's cave, but they got banished for frightening Monstro City's residents. Ssh! Tonight they've flapped back for a secret visit.

How many bats are hanging from the roof?
Write the total here.

Can you spot poor, over-run Ecto?
Draw a circle round the Spooky.

There's one other Moshling lurking in the twilight. Who is it?

···

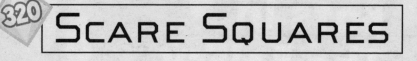

SCARE SQUARES

THESE SCARE SQUARES ARE ABOUT AS TERRIFYING AS CUTE KISSY GETS! HELP THE BABY GHOST COUNT THE NUMBER OF SQUARES FLOATING AROUND THIS PAGE.

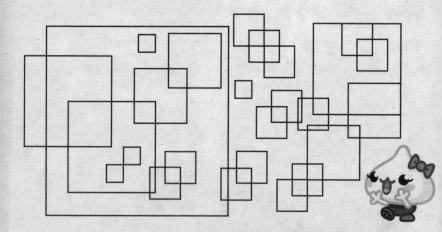

321 Trouble On The High Seas

It's not about cocktails on deck or dinner at the captain's table when you're a monster pirate - Cap'n Buck's trusty crew are sailing into the eye of a storm! There's so much rain and wind it's hard to tell what's what. Ahoy landlubber, study the scene with an eyeglass then write in this pirate puzzle log.

1. Which Moshling is on the upper sail?

....

2. Who is at the wheel?

....

3. How many Birdies are in the crew?

....

4. Which Spookie is on board and what's different about it?

....

5. Who is keeping lookout from the crow's nest?

....

6. How many portholes can you spy? ....

Telescopic Dot-to-Dot

Buster Bumblechops is relentless in his quest to bag elusive new Moshlings. He's searched far and wide, but the critters can pop up in the unlikeliest places. Who is in Buster's sights now? Join up the dots to find out.

25 • — • 1   2 •   3 •
                           4 •
24 •
                               • 5
23 •
20 • 21 • 22 •   • 6
        • 15   7 •   • 9
19 • 16 •   13 • 8 • 10
18 17   14 12
              11 •

Can you guess?

....

Tricky Trivia

It's time to rummage about in your brain and dig out all those random factoids you collect without even thinking. How quick are you at quizzing? You've got thirty seconds to put your general knowledge to the test - ready, set, go!

1. What is water made of?

☐ Carbon

☐ Nitrogen

☐ Oxygen and Carbon

☐ Oxygen and Hydrogen

2. Which of these peoples did not invade the British Isles?

☐ The Egyptians

☐ The Romans

☐ The Anglo Saxons

☐ The Vikings

3. What is the nearest star to Earth?

☐ Saturn

☐ Mars

☐ The Sun

☐ Pluto

4. What is one hundred years?

☐ A Decade

☐ A Century

☐ An Anniversary

☐ A Millenium

5. What is the capital city of Norway?

☐ Gothenburg

☐ Copenhagen

☐ Stockholm

☐ Oslo

Time taken...........................

Score ....

Snoop Dawg

Psst! What do you know about McNulty, the most secretive Puppy Moshling? Find a quiet spot, then tick your way through the choices in this quiz. Don't get hoodwinked by the phoney answers - only the smartest Moshis will suss all eight!

1. Does McNulty hail from...
Sherlock Nook or Watson Warren?

2. Is McNulty known as...
The Musky Husky or the Undercover Yap Yap?

3. Is McNulty skilled at...
Squeezing into tiny spaces or disguising himself?

4. Is McNulty's favourite hat a...
Trilby or a Deerstalker?

5. The things that bug this Moshling the most are...
Muddy paw prints and wire coat hangers or CCTV and invisible ink?

6. The best way to crack a McNulty in disguise is to...
Listen for panting noises or look for the very waggy tail?

7. The seeds to attract McNulty are...
A Star Blossom and two Snap Apples or a Star Blossom and two Magic Beans?

8. The Puppy's eyes are a...
fetching shade of blue or a gorgeous poochy green?

Lop-sided Lookout

It would be nice to describe this pirate as 'having good sea legs', but it would also be totally untrue! An unfortunate sword fight with a seagull has relegated the unlucky swabber to a permanent spot in the crow's nest. Who is he?

R	A	S	P	A	N	C	Q	O	M
B	M	I	H	Q	H	R	B	A	J
H	J	A	S	G	D	G	Z	P	F
I	I	D	C	E	V	A	A	Z	C
S	P	I	U	P	W	U	P	G	P
O	I	T	G	K	G	I	R	J	I
N	B	P	A	R	M	W	L	B	H
J	I	A	S	C	V	A	X	I	G
C	Z	D	B	I	G	R	S	K	X
N	H	D	Y	O	S	D	O	S	A

Work out the sailor's name by crossing out the letters that appear more than once in this grid.

Captain Buck's crewman is ....

Waldo's Wacky Word Box

How will you fare this time? Are you getting quicker? Are they getting easier? Perhaps Waldo is making your grey matter melt with the very effort of solving his grids? Answer each of the Tabby Nerdicat's clues, writing the words both vertically and horizontally onto the grid.

	1	2	3	4
1				
2				
3				
4				

CLUES

1. Walk in shallow water.

2. The highest point.

3. When you feel you've experienced something before. _ _ _ _ -vu.

4. Test.

Remember to write each answer across as well as down!

Alphabet Soup

OK puzzle peeps, I'll let this loony letter quiz do the talking. Can you rattle through the questions in less than half a minute? See you on the other side!

1. Which vowel is missing from this alphabet?

A ☐   E ☐
O ☐   U ☐

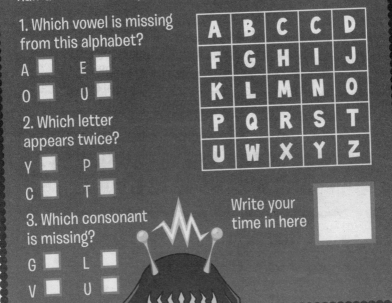

A	B	C	C	D
F	G	H	I	J
K	L	M	N	O
P	Q	R	S	T
U	W	X	Y	Z

2. Which letter appears twice?

Y ☐   P ☐
C ☐   T ☐

3. Which consonant is missing?

G ☐   L ☐
V ☐   U ☐

Write your time in here ☐

Rapid Rhyme

Who the devil could be hiding here?
Read the riddle, then puzzle it out!

**I'm feisty and sneaky, and quite fiery too,
My head's full of lava, I sizzle, I do!
Happy and cheeky, we'll get on great,
Choose me for your room and you'll have a top mate!**

Who am I?

WHAT'S THE STORE-Y?

The storeowners of Monstro City are a tight-knit group. After a day's trading, Dewy and his pals often meet up over a flagon of snail ale to share tips and motivate each other. How many positive words and phrases can you make from this inspiring Moshi mantra?

'MONSTERS ARE MY BUSINESS AND BUSINESS IS GOOD!'

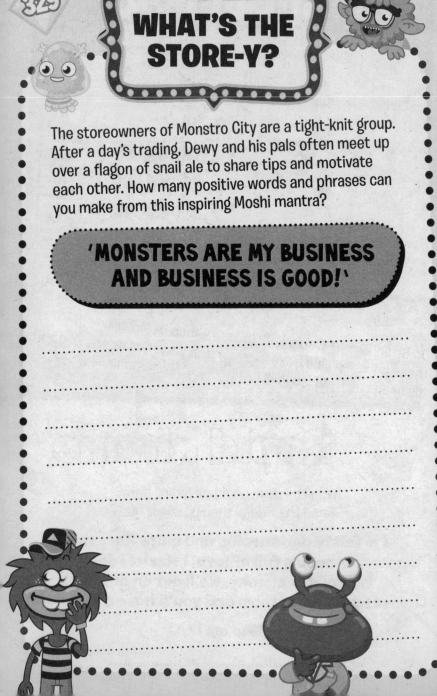

Master Of Moshi

Which of the following is not a genu-ine winnable Moshi Medal?

BRANIAC ☐
GLUMP GRABBER ☐
AWESOME ADOPTER ☐
D.I.Y. DESIGNER ☐

chock-a-block

Dr. Strangeglove would love to trap a mob of Moshlings in these impenetrable boxes. In fact, the very idea makes him throw his head back and laugh in wicked glee. Mwah-hahahahahah!

Count up the portable prisons, then write down exactly how many the villain has here.

Write your answer in here. ☐

Spookies Quiz

There's nothing to be scared of about this bunch of Moshlings. In fact, they're all rather cool. Did you know that Spookies can plop out of plasma clouds and drift through walls? Use this quiz to probe your knowledge even more.

1. What is Big Bad Bill's favourite food?
A. Ghoul-ash ☐
B. Rat Tail Spaghetti ☐
C. Deep Fried Oobla Doobla ☐

2. What type of Moshling is Ecto?
A. A Fancy Banshee ☐
B. A Green Ghostie ☐
C. A Heebee Jeebee ☐

3. Which part of the body might you want to hide from Squidge?
A. Your bottom ☐
B. Your neck ☐
C. Your nose ☐

4. What does Big Bad Bill always carry with him?
A. A set of fake fangs ☐
B. A skull-topped staff ☐
C. A cape ☐

5. What is Kissy's favourite bedtime story?
A. *Beauty and the Beastie* ☐
B. *Ghouldilocks and the Three Bears* ☐
C. *Cutie-Pie'd Piper* ☐

6. Which Spookie loves collecting Rox dust?
A. Kissy ☐
B. Big Bad Bill ☐
C. Ecto ☐

7. Where do Kissys come from?
A. The plasma clouds above the Okay-ish lands ☐
B. The trees in the Gombala Gombala Jungle ☐
C. A parallel vortex within the ClothEar Clouds ☐

8. What are the rarest Spookies?
A. Woolly Blue Hoodoos ☐
B. Baby Ghosts ☐
C. Furry Heebees ☐

READER'S DIGEST

Poor Prof. Purplex! His appetite for scoffing books leaves much to be desired . . . and not much left on the shelves. He's currently banned from every library in the land! Only one bookstore didn't get the message. Now the Owl of Wiseness has sneaked in and started munching there too.

How many books are there for Prof. Purplex to munch?

Spot the Speedy Difference

Wow, not bad for an old guy! Buster Bumblechops can really rocket when he's in hot pursuit of an errant Moshling. Here he's donned turbo-powered skates in his quest to catch Cutie Pie. Can you spot six differences between the two pictures?

Here's another of Blurp's 'say what you see' puzzles. Each of these boxed puzzles hides a saying, place or common catchphrase. Don't just read the letters, think about how they're placed.

1. S E O G T A H W (↑)

MUSTCOME (↓)

2. 1 END 3 END 5 END 7 END 9 END

3. LOOK BE BE BE BE U LEAP

4. N W O R G

5. C
—————
CAVE

6. ENO ERAUQS OT

Dinos in the Dark

The Friendly Tree Woods are welcoming by day, but by night it gets so dark you can't see your hand in front of your face or a Glump under your galoshes. Which Dinos are lurking in the shadows tonight? Draw lines to the blank boxes and then write the Moshling names in each.

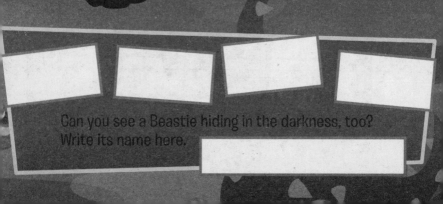

Can you see a Beastie hiding in the darkness, too? Write its name here.

BLOCK PARTY

The Diavlo in the centre of this map has got so incensed with the traffic, he's shed lava everywhere! Can you help the mad Moshi find his way out of this busy neighbourhood? Put your finger on Diavlo. Now move him four blocks east, two blocks south and another block east. Where does he end up? Draw a circle around the letter marking his destination.

Gardeners' Question Time

If you want to grab a few moments peace, head out back to your Moshling Garden. It's the grow-to destination for Moshis that want to lure a Moshling. Can you answer these questions about the greenest place around?

1. How many seed patches are there in the garden?

....

2. Which tiny creature often zooms up and down the tree trunk?

....

3. What are the scarecrow's eyes made out of?

....

4. How many patches are on the scarecrow's tunic?

....

5. What lies between the door of the building and the window?

....

6. Which bird-like character perches in the tree?

....

Tricky Trivia

This is one of the hardest zoology exams a Moshi Monster can sit - luckily, you should ace this test. Set your timer to thirty seconds, then tick the correct answer to each triv teaser.

What is the human body's biggest organ?

THE SKIN ☐
THE HEART ☐
THE LUNGS ☐
THE KIDNEYS ☐

What are the bones that make up your fingers called?

VERTEBRAE ☐
HUMERUS ☐
PHALANGES ☐
TIBIA ☐

What is the substance that gives hair and skin its pigment called?

KERATIN ☐
MELANIN ☐
BLEACH ☐
KEROSENE ☐

How many bones does the adult human body have?

JUST OVER 500 BONES ☐
JUST OVER 300 BONES ☐
JUST OVER 200 BONES ☐
JUST OVER 100 BONES ☐

As well as allowing you to hear, what else do the ears help control?

BREATHING ☐
ABILITY TO SPEAK ☐
BALANCE ☐
HAIR GROWTH ☐

Vowel Howl

Chop Chop might be a total joker, but he's not the brightest Moshling in the Monstroverse. He'd probably stop cackling the second you asked him the answer to this puzzle!

Which of these words has its vowels in exactly the same place as the word at the top. You have fifteen seconds to beat the Cheeky Chimp to the answer!

JOKER

BADLY ☐ **BEACH** ☐

BUSES ☐ **BANJO** ☐

Seagull's love to squawk, but if you really listened you'd know they're actually quite tuneful. Here's a little self-titled ditty written by one of The Port's happiest inhabitants. Can you guess who it is? He's often screeching - soz, singing - it to himself.

SUPER TOUGH!

A bird am I, but no 'Birdie',

A gull who really loves the sea,

I check for baddies in The Port,

No villains please, of any sort,

I wear a patch upon my eye,

But please don't ask the

reason why,

I'm neither hurt nor on the mend,

It's 'cos it is the latest trend.

Who am I?

SNEAKY SNAKES

Stacey Grace is late for school again because she can't tie her shoelaces. As well as tripping over a lot, it also probably explains why she couldn't do this puzzle homework set by her teacher Miss Jingle. Can you help her? Study the six stretchy serpents, then put a star next to the one that is the longest.

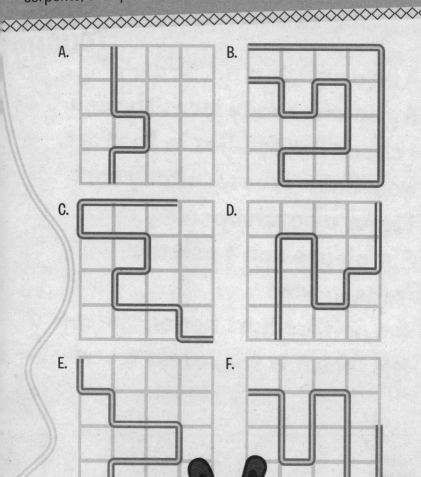

Crack the Ken Ken

Ooh, puzzlers! This twisted take on Sudoku has been such a hit here in Monstro City. Ready to give this Ken Ken your best shot?

The aim is to fill each horizontal and vertical line of the box with the digits 1 to 4. The numbers must all appear once only in each line. The numbers in each cage must add up to the small digit in the corner of the cell by the mathematical means stated. Happy Ken Kening!

It's For You-HOO!

Look who's just been recharging in Voltage Vaults! This gaggle of chatting Gabbys are tingalinging with excitement! Can you count up the Mini Moshifones?

Write the correct answer here.

NIFTY SHIFTY

Tubby Huggishis are so squeezable, but there are occasions when you might want to give them a wide berth. Purdy has a rather messy pastime. Can you work out what it is by shifting each letter one place forward?

CHOOHMF SGDHQ OZVR HM RXQTO

_____ _____ _____ ___ _____

Lilo Len!

Poor ole Lenny Lard is still trying to learn to swim. Can you help him navigate through the Islands? There's only one route that will take him out into the big wide ocean.

346

Finish

A
B
C
D
E

Moshling Muddle

Monstro City would grind to a halt without these tireless workers! Which three Roarkers have got mixed up in this grid?

The Roarkers are...

1. .... 2. ....

3. ....

ZZZZZZZZZZZZZZZZ

Who's catching some Zzzzs on this page? Hazard a guess, then fill in three key facts about this snoozy Moshling.

ZZZZZZZZZZZZZZZZZZZZZZ

His Moshling number is ....
His personality could be described as ....
One of his dislikes is ....

349 Eyes Spy 👀

When Shelley Splurt is oozing along the Underground Tunnels, all you can see are her eyes! This test will help you refine your peeper-spotting skills. Can you count how many eyeballs are blinking on this page?

Write the total
in this box.

BIRDIES QUIZ

Chirp, chirp, tweet, tweet, techno, techno, Techno, TECHNO!
Did you know that apart from beaks, wings and feathers, the only thing that these Moshlings have in common is their commitment to an annual event - the Birdie Bash.

'Come again?' you say. It's true! The Birdie Bash is a crazy rave hosted by Disco Duckies on the Taki Taki Islands. Sounds fun? Here's your plus one invite - provided you can answer all of the questions below!

1. What do Disco Duckies use to slick back their feathers?
A. Orange Sauce
B. Plum Sauce
C. Neon Soup

2. What type of Moshling is Peppy?
A. A Pirate Penguin
B. A Biker Penguin
C. A Stunt Penguin

3. What do Pilfering Toucans most like stealing from other Moshlings?
A. Rox
B. Their Moshling pals
C. Salty Gobstoppers

4. Who has a strange affection for plinky toy pianos?
A. Prof. Purplex
B. DJ Quack
C. Peppy

5.

What strange thing sets Peppy apart from other Birdies?

A. He doesn't attend the Birdie Bash

B. He can't fly

C. He has very sharp teeth

6.

Where did all Birdie species once dwell together?

A. On the Frosty Pop Glacier
B. Wobbly Woods
C. Fluttertown - an ancient tree village

7.

Which is the only species of Birdie that is not rare?

A. Tiki
B. Peppy
C. DJ Quack

8.

What is the seed code to catch Peppy?

A. Moon Orchid (Any), Moon Orchid (Red), Magic Beans (Yellow)

B. Moon Orchid (Any), Dragon Fruit (Any), Star Blossom (Any)

C. Star Blossom (Any), Love Berries (Pink), Love Berries (Red)

Who knew?!
Back in the day, Disco Duckies were known as Classical Quackers!

WHO'S IN THE FROGGIE SUIT?

Naughty, naughty! Someone's tugged on Scamp's pink bow and undone her bouncy Froggie outfit. Now they're trying it on for size! With just their eyes, nose and mouth showing, can you tell who the culprit is?

Write your answer here

....

Why not see how a froggie suit looks on your fave Moshling? Draw their face in here.

Pony Pluses

These huggable horsey Moshlings used to be ridden by monsters, before some clever Moshi invented the wheel. Use your potty Ponies knowledge to answer the maths questions below. Can you write in all of the numbers then work out the sum?

The number of species of Pony
MULTIPLIED BY
The number of Ponies with a horn
MINUS
The number of wings on Angel
DIVIDED BY
The number of Hot Silly Pepper Seeds needed to catch a Mr Snoodle
PLUS
The total number of legs when all the Pony species are added up
PLUS
The number of Ponies with rainbow-striped manes and tails

= ....

SUPER TOUGH!

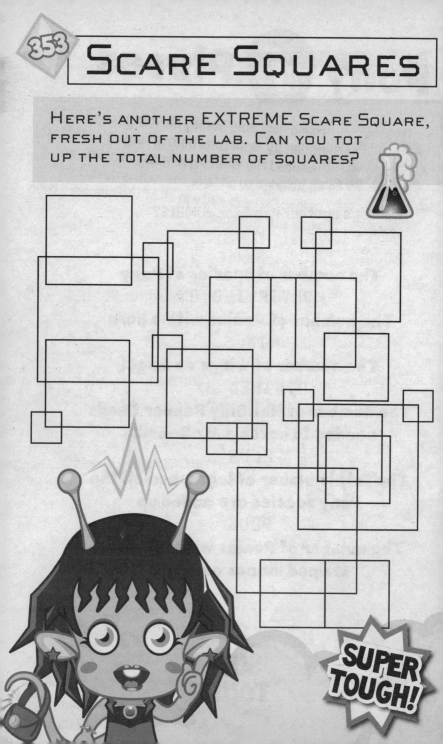

353

SCARE SQUARES

HERE'S ANOTHER EXTREME SCARE SQUARE, FRESH OUT OF THE LAB. CAN YOU TOT UP THE TOTAL NUMBER OF SQUARES?

SUPER TOUGH!

WORD WARP

Don't freak! This Zommer only wants to try
and bag a decent score at the Word Warp challenge.
Read each word, then tick the word underneath it that
shares the same meaning.

1. What's another word for JUMBLE?

MUDDLE ☐　　MUMBLE ☐

PATCHES ☐　　JUGGLE ☐

2. What's another word for SCARE?

TICKLE ☐　　FRIGHTEN ☐

JUMP ☐　　JOLT ☐

3. What's another word for DRIBBLE?

SMIRK ☐　　GRIN ☐

SPLATTER ☐　　DROOL ☐

4. What's another word for STITCH?

TACK ☐　　TIE ☐

STICK ☐　　KNOT ☐

5. What's another word for ODD?

NORMAL ☐

PLOD ☐

STRANGE ☐

UNKNOWN ☐

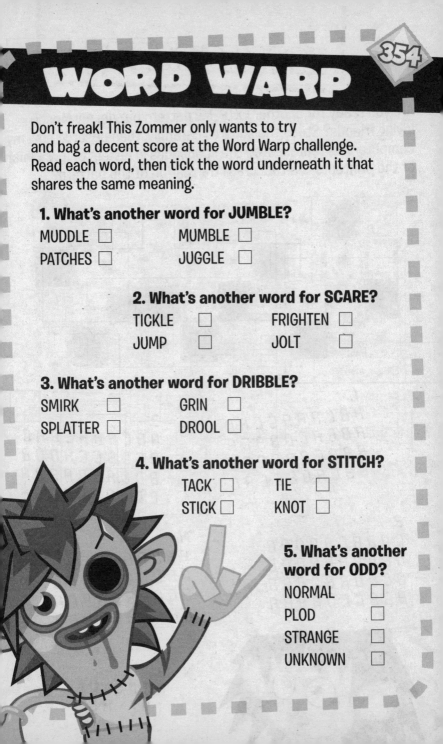

MANIC MATCH

Are you ready for another EXTREME pattern puzzle, my Moshi-loving friends? Study the squares carefully, then observe how my computer has represented the sequences in letters below. Which of the printouts is an accurate translation of the pattern?

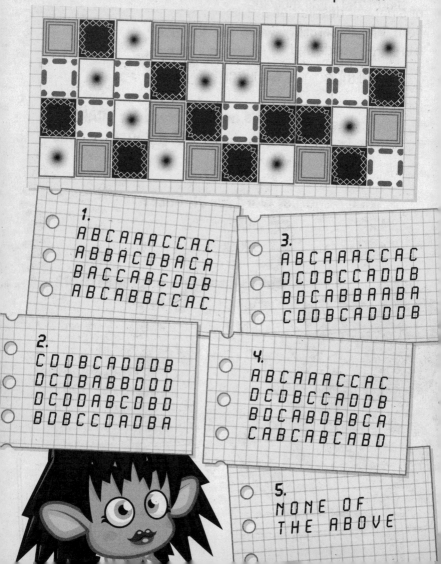

1.
```
ABCAAACCAC
ABBACDBACA
BACCABCDDB
ABCABBCCAC
```

3.
```
ABCAAACCAC
DCDBCCADDB
BDCABBAABA
CDDBCADDDB
```

2.
```
CDDBCADDDB
DCDBABBDDD
DCDDABCDBD
BDBCCDADBA
```

4.
```
ABCAAACCAC
DCDBCCADDB
BDCABDBBCA
CABCABCABD
```

5.
```
NONE OF
THE ABOVE
```

356

Members Only

This coded spiral holds the name of a popular destination at The Port. Can you crack it? Start from the outside and work in, circling every fifth letter.

joizPzsMLaINBuWBY7AShf23AgFkoNliVPPPcs9CAT7vLLBPLAO9juWSqUESjeTB4t3tTYA76...

Now write the letters in order below.

_ _ _ _ _   _ _ _   _ _ _ _ _ _

POTTY PATTERNS

Check out all the cute critters lined up in a row! Completing each of these patterns requires an awesome combination of cool doodling skills and Moshling knowledge.
First choose the right names from the bottom of the page to label each picture.
Now fill the blanks in with your own mini-Moshling sketches.

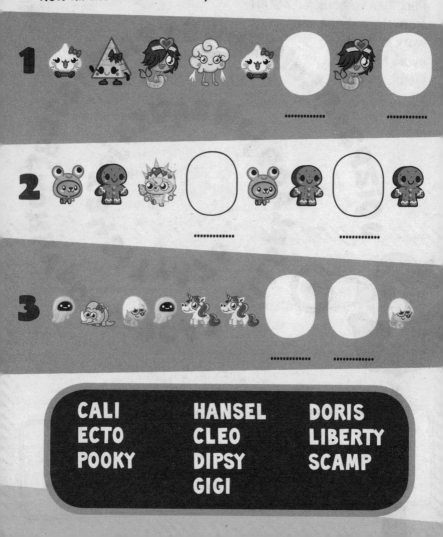

1

2

3

CALI   HANSEL   DORIS
ECTO   CLEO   LIBERTY
POOKY   DIPSY   SCAMP
           GIGI

Bubble Trouble

How can something so floaty, pretty and light be soooooo frustrating? Peer closely at this batch of bubbles, then reach for a pencil and start puzzling.

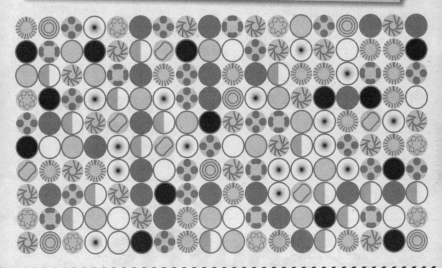

1. Which bubble appears least? ....

2. How many white bubbles are there? ....

3. How many bubbles are there with a black dot in the middle? ....

4. Which type of bubble isn't touching a white bubble?

....

5. Which bubble only appears on the sides of the grid? ....

SUPER TOUGH!

359

Bye Bye Batty Boxes

Here's batty old Blurp's last batch of brainteasers. This time the Bubblefish has upped the ante! Look at each box and repeat what you see. Don't over-think things – in this quiz your first answer is the most likely to be the right one.

1.
ABCDEFGHI
JKMNOPQR
STUVWXYZ

360

Shuffle Kerfuffle

G N R I U G A M M

2.

E C

  D

A N

3. *100 MPH BANANAS*
90 MPH CHEESE
85 MPH DOUGHNUTS

4. ☑ FEZ
☐ TRILBY
☐ SOMBRERO
☐ CAP
☐ BERET

Gossipy, Fluffle-loving and nosy, this Moshling has a penchant for Moon Orchids of all colours. What type of monster pet could it be? Unshuffle the letters to find out!

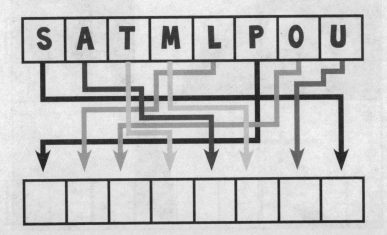

S	A	T	M	L	P	O	U

Super Colour Copy

The only thing better than a Moshi Monster is a Super Moshi Monster! Check out this caped Furi. Doesn't he look awesome? Now draw him yourself by carefully copying each of the squares into the right place on the empty grid.

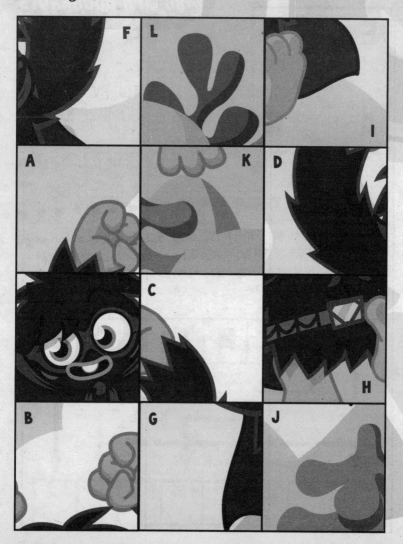

A

B

C

D

E

F

G

H

I

J

K

L

Crazy Quilt

Kind old Buster really cares about his Moshlings. He often makes quilts to wrap up Fiery Frazzledragons that are feeling the cold. Unfortunately the blankets only tend to last five minutes before Burnie accidentally sets fire to them. Perhaps the Moshling Hunter will have more luck with this kind of quilt!

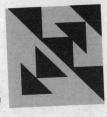

A

B

C

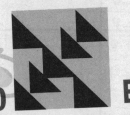

D

E

Only one of these squares has a tiny flaw in it - can you help Buster locate it?

F

Barbecued Bubblefish, this page is teeming with ultra rare Moshlings! The sight is enough to make Buster Bumblechops' eyes water. Eleven words associated with these exotic critters are hidden in the wordsearch square. Can you find each and every one?

G	H	F	L	A	S	H	Y	F	O	X	G
N	V	Y	T	B	L	B	C	G	Q	W	R
I	V	W	U	R	L	Y	G	E	D	L	E
P	N	J	P	H	I	V	D	M	N	L	P
S	I	F	G	O	H	B	N	Y	G	I	P
N	G	F	T	G	A	D	Z	R	X	B	I
I	G	S	M	N	T	V	U	B	M	D	N
B	Y	Q	O	I	S	G	Q	G	Y	A	L
K	I	I	P	L	P	F	X	D	X	B	L
C	U	S	T	B	I	N	D	G	O	G	F
A	K	P	O	J	H	B	V	D	R	I	K
Z	P	R	P	J	K	X	S	O	T	B	H

☐ ZACK BINSPIN
☐ ROXY
☐ BLINGO
☐ NIPPER
☐ BIG BAD BILL
☐ IGGY
☐ WURLY

☐ HIPSTA HILLS
☐ MOPTOP
☐ FLASHY FOX
☐ GURGLE

BLOCK PARTY

Aaah! This Kissy's feeling a little disorientated after dropping out of a plasma cloud. Can you help her get her bearings?

Put your pinkie on the spooky Moshling - go on, don't be scared! Now move her three blocks east, one block north, another one block east and four blocks south. Where does she end up? Draw a circle around the letter marking her destination.

	E						A
	A		F		A		C
	D		A	C	B		
B		A	B	F		E	
B	A	F		B	D		
	B	C	E	A	F		
D			C		C		E
	A					A	D

Ode to a Persistent Puzzler

Can there be any grey matter left in those brain banks? What a workout! Congratulations on a stackload of EXTREME puzzle action - if anyone's earned themselves a slice of Roarberry Cheesecake and a cup of Mr. Tea, it's you! Now relax, put your feet up and complete the blanks in my farewell poem.

It's Tamara again, sure you know me by now,
If you don't recognise me I'd say to you 'How?'
I hope you've enjoyed my conundrums within,
To leave ones unanswered would just be a _ _ _ ,
So make sure you've puzzled and worked through this book,
If you've missed pages then go back and _ _ _ _ ,
Once you have reached this point, puzzler I fear,
You've come to the end of another long _ _ _ _ ,
But you'll have learnt logic and patience and such,
By doing these puzzles, So thanks very _ _ _ _ ,
Bye now Moshi fan, thanks for your time,
Well done on completing this rather long _ _ _ _ _ .

ANSWERS

Puzzle 1
PONY PICKS

A	S	E	L	P	P	A	Y	D	N	A	C
C	L	O	U	D	N	I	N	E	Q	U	I
M	G	A	N	G	R	A	N	G	E	L	W
A	D	L	V	E	I	J	O	L	K	I	L
G	A	L	T	E	N	G	D	X	N	F	U
I	N	I	G	R	R	O	I	G	E	G	F
C	N	C	F	B	O	R	S	U	J	B	E
A	D	S	P	N	N	S	O	E	T	U	C
L	O	I	S	M	G	L	E	E	B	H	A
S	A	R	A	I	T	I	E	T	A	A	R
K	M	P	C	X	V	A	N	L	T	R	G
X	H	A	U	G	H	T	Y	G	E	E	L

Puzzle 2
WILD WORD CHALLENGE
There's a stack of words you could have come up with, but here's a dozen for starters . . .
Melt, vet, trip, Luvli, plume, sell, metre, veil, sleep, multiplex, serve, trill, (and the BEST of all . . .) repulverise

Puzzle 3
MOSHI JUMBLE

1. Luvli
2. Poppet
3. Katsuma

Puzzle 4
SPOOKY SUDOKU

Puzzle 5
NAUGHTY NINJA!
9

Puzzle 6
PURPLEXING PUZZLE
41, 51, 66 and 81.

Puzzle 7
EYES SPY
54

Puzzle 8
GROSS-ERY GIGGLES
Snozzle Wobbleson

Puzzle 9
MYSTERY MOSHLING

I'm Blurp, the Batty Bubblefish

Puzzle 10
MOSHLING MEMORY GAME
1. 5, 2. 2, 3. Purdy, 4. It's had a bite taken out of it, 5. 2, 6. Kissy.

Puzzle 12
ODD ODDIE OUT
Oddie F must go

Puzzle 13
SCARE SQUARES
38

Puzzle 14
BUBBLE TROUBLE
1. 12, 2. , 3. , 4. 13, 5.

Puzzle 15
GLUMPS CROSSWORD

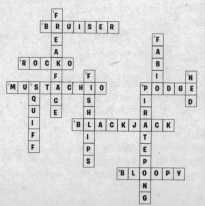

Page 16
COUNTRY CODE
Cadged a Fab Badge

Puzzle 17
FUN PARK FREAKOUT
B

Puzzle 18
FACT OR FIB?
1. Fact, 2. Fact, 3. Fib. It's Giuseppe Gelato the Ice-Scream Man, 4. Fib. He's Moshling mad!, 5. Fib. It's Dr. Strangeglove, 6. Fact, 7. Fib. They are at Candy Shoals, 8. Fact

Puzzle 19
BLOCK PARTY
E

Puzzle 20
HERE FISHIE FISHIE

		¹S	E	A	S	T	A	R		
²F	R	U	I	T	F	A	L	L	S	
	³O	C	E	A	N					
		⁴S	A	N	D	W	I	C	H	E	S
			⁵G	L	O	O	P			
			⁶B	L	E	U	R	G	H	
⁷V	A	L	L	E	Y	M	E	R	M	A	I	D

Puzzle 21
LINE DANCE
20

Puzzle 22
CHOCK-A-BLOCK
127

Puzzle 23
CRAZY QUILT
H

Puzzle 24
TRICKY TRIVIA
1. Binspin, 2. Sweet Tooth, 3. Babs' Boutique, 4. Tyra Fangs, 5. Serve at the Ice-Scream! store, 6. Poppet.

Puzzle 25
BUSHY'S SOCK BONANZA
The answer is four. Although there are many socks in the drawer, there are only three colours, so if you take four socks then you are guaranteed to have at least one matching pair!

Puzzle 26
BREAK THE BLOCKS
The central 1x1x1 block has six faces. Any cut can only reveal one of these faces, so six cuts are needed, and also are enough.

Puzzle 27
VILE VOWELS
1. BREAK-IN AT HORRODS: DR. STRANGEGLOVE SUSPECTED!
2. VOLCANO ERUPTION THREATENS MONSTRO CITY
3. RESIDENTS IN UPROAR OVER 'PONGY' PIRATE GLUMP NEIGHBOUR
4. MOE YUKKY REGAINS GOLDEN MOP TROPHY
5. TYRA FANGS AND ROARY SCRAWL TO WED IN SECRET CEREMONY?

Puzzle 28
MOSHLING TREATS
You give a Swirlberry Muffin to each of your first nine Moshlings, and the basket with a muffin in it to the tenth Moshling. Each Moshling has a treat, but one has their Swirlberry Muffin in a basket!

Puzzle 29
BEANIE BLOB BARGAIN
You could buy eleven Beanie Blobs, leaving just 1 Rox in your wallet!

Puzzle 30
FINE FURNISHINGS
1. FLUTTERBY CABINET, 2. FOOT TABLE,
3. FRIED EGG RUG, 4. MAGIC MIRROR,
5. GREEN SLIME WALLPAPER,
6. SURFBOARD DOOR

Puzzle 31
WORLDIE ONE OUT
1. Cleo, 2. Raarghly. He is not a Worldie, or even a Moshling! (Raarghly is a rare monster from outer space.)
3. Rocky, 4. Mini Ben, 5. Liberty.

Puzzle 32
ROX 'N' ROLL

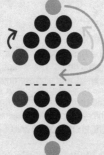

Start by moving the top Rox to the bottom. Now move the far left Rox on the row of four up two levels, to turn the row of two into a row of three Rox. Finally move the far right Rox from the bottom row up two levels to make a new row of four Rox. Ta-da!

Puzzle 33
LINE DANCE
12

Puzzle 34
SPARKLEPOP BRAIN BURP
The fourth band member is Coolio himself!

Puzzle 35
ADE IT UP!
Roland drinks four bottles an hour, ninety-six in a day and 672 in a week.

Puzzle 36
SIX SNEAKY SNAKES
E

Puzzle 37
HAPPY SWITCHY DAY!
1. SWITCHY BALLOONS, 2. SWITCHY STORMY WALLPAPER, 3. HUMAN FACE PARTS, 4. SWITCHY FAIRY CAKE, 5. TYRE SWING, 6. UN-SMILEY FLOWERS

Puzzle 38
MANIC MATCH
4 is correct

Puzzle 39
SUPER SCRAMBLE
A. SLUDGE FUDGE, B. KATSUMA, C. FLUTTERBY FIELD, D. MOSHLINGOLOGY

Puzzle 40
GAME ON

Puzzle 41
BERT ALERT!

Puzzle 42
MOSHLING SPELLING TEST
FIEND is the correct answer.

LOLIPOP	LOLLIPOP
MONSTEROUS	MONSTROUS
WIERD	WEIRD
GROSE	GROSS
DISSAPEAR	DISAPPEAR
HOWEL	HOWL
RYHTHEM	RHYTHM

Puzzle 43
GIVE US A CLUEKOO!
C

Puzzle 44
SCARE SQUARES
41

Puzzle 45
MOSHLING ZOO
A. Purdy, B. Priscilla, C. Pooky, D. Honey,
E. Plinky, F. Peppy
Honey is the odd-Moshling-out because her name doesn't begin with 'P'.

Puzzle 46
C.L.ON.C. CODE
CRIMINAL LEAGUE OF NAUGHTY CRITTERS

Puzzle 47
A STROLL DOWN SLUDGE STREET
1. The DIY shop, 2. Eco Adventure, Bug's Big Bounce, Sea Monster Munch or Weevil Kneevil's Downhill Dash, 3. Zommer 4. Dodgy Dealz, 5. Horrods, 6. The cows (Chomper and Stomper), 7. D.I.Y. Shop, 8. The Volcano, 9. Billy Bob Baitman, 10. A money bag with a Rox symbol on the front

Puzzle 48
DOODLE ISLAND

Puzzle 49
WHO'S HAT IS THAT?
1. D, 2. B, 3. A, 4. F, 5. E, 6. C.

Puzzle 50
LINE DANCE
13

Puzzle 51
PORT REPORT
A-harrr! I looked through my telescope and I did see a fishing boat with three **flags** fluttering at the stern. On the water, I spied **three** rowing boats, sculling across the water. One of the boats had a **seagull** perched on the brow. There were a pair of wooden **barrels** there too, bobbing up and down on the beautiful briny sea. Made me want to dive in meself! I looked out for Mr Meowford's trawler, but I would wager that he **wasn't out** this morning. Suddenly a **periscope** rose out of the shallows and peeped back at me. Could there be a submarine cruising round this port of mine? I turned my glass to the sky and counted a shoal of **five** flying fish. The weather was **rainy**. A good day for seafarin'!

Puzzle 52
TRICKY TRIVIA
1. Holland, 2. *Chamber of Secrets*, 3. Calf, 4. A painter, 5. One half.

Puzzle 53
NOSHWORD PUZZLE

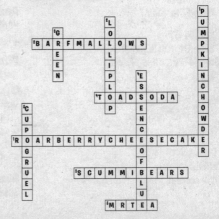

Puzzle 54
EYES SPY
50

Puzzle 55
CATCH THE CURSER
THE PORT, GIFT ISLAND
OOH LA LANE, MAIN STREET
SLUDGE STREET, VOLCANO

Puzzle 56
BUSTER BUMBLECHOPS' CAMERA
Big Bad Bill, Gigi, Mini Ben, Oddie

Puzzle 57
ONCE UPON A MOSHI - PART I

Chapter 1	Even
Chapter 2	36 Rox
Chapter 3	50 kilos
Chapter 4	400 bricks
Chapter 5	6 hours

Puzzle 58
I SHOULD KEN KEN

6+ 4	3+ 2	1	3
2	3- 4	7+ 3	3+ 1
3	1	4	2
4+ 1	3	2- 2	4

Puzzle 59
NIFTY SHIFTY
ELMORE THE GREAT

Puzzle 61
I SCREAM, YOU SCREAM, WE ALL
SCREAM FOR ICE-SCREAM!
13

Puzzle 62
PEEK-A-POOKY
C

Puzzle 63
ONCE UPON A MOSHI - PART II

Chapter 6	2 hours
Chapter 7	8 hours longer - so he worked twice as long
Chapter 8	60 Rox
Chapter 9	30 square metres left over
Chapter 10	10 Rox in fifth month

Puzzle 64
DOUBLE-CROSSER

 It's Burnie

Puzzle 65
CHOCK-A-BLOCK
134

Puzzle 66
ICKLE LIMERICK
Chop Chop the
Cheeky Chimp

Puzzle 67
LET SLEEPING SNUFFLERS LIE
1. Snooze Cruise, 2. Mr Snoodle
3. Humphrey, 4. Stashley Snoozer

Puzzle 69
HANSEL'S SWEET STASH
24

Puzzle 70
ONCE UPON A MOSHI - PART III

Chapter 11	20 metres
Chapter 12	3 hours later
Chapter 13	7 am
Chapter 14	They ate 18, leaving 32 in the bag
Chapter 15	12 kilometres

Puzzle 71
SKEETER'S SHORT CUT
F

Puzzle 72
STICKY STUCKY IN THE MUCKY
TIKI, SNOOKUMS, PRISCILLA, BLURP

Puzzle 73
BUBBLE TROUBLE
1. 3, 2. 🌀, 3. 49, 4. ◉, 5. 🌀

Puzzle 74
OH 'ECK! IT'S ECTO
25

Puzzle 75
WACKY TRACK
DJ **Quack's** a Disco Duckie,
He'll boogie for you, if you're very **lucky,**
His favourite **move/step/dance** is the Moonwalk,
Don't step on his feet 'cos it makes him **squawk.**

Puzzle 76
WHAT'S IN STORE?

Gilbert Finnster	Paws 'n' Claws
Mizz Snoots	Horrods
Bushy Fandango	Bizarre Bazaar
Dewy	DIY Shop
Snozzle Wobbleson	Gross-ery Store
Moe Yukky	Yukea

Puzzle 77
LUCKY NUMBERS
13, 26, 39, 52, 65, 78, 91, 104, 117, 130, 143, 156

Puzzle 78
ONCE UPON A MOSHI – PART IV

Chapter 16	Half a kilometre
Chapter 17	180 seconds
Chapter 18	49 years old
Chapter 19	4 Rox per kilo
Chapter 20	3,750 Rox

Puzzle 79
WORD WARP
1. Soar, 2. Twinkle, 3. Weird
4. Contented, 5. Enchantment

Puzzle 80
MOSHI MASH-UP

1. PUPPY + MARE	PUMA
2. CRAB + OWL	CROW
3. HAWK + REINDEER	HARE
4. MONKEY + THRUSH	MOTH
5. SEAGULL + ALLIGATOR	SEAL
6. WALLABY + SPIDER	WASP
7. TURTLE + NAWHARL	TUNA
8. BUFFALO + LLAMA	BULL

Puzzle 81
HAPPY SNAPPIES
1. Cuddly humans, 2. Cherry Bomb
3. The Moshi Monstars, 4. Yukea

Puzzle 82
TRICKY TRIVIA
1. 1939, 2. Sunday, 3. Canberra, 4. Mandarin Chinese, 5. Alexander Graham Bell

Puzzle 83
LIGHTS OUT!
1. Diavlo, 2. Katsuma, 3. Luvli
4. Zommer, 5. Poppet, 6. Furi

Puzzle 84
BLOCK PARTY
C

Puzzle 85
MYTH OR MUMBO JUMBO?
1. True, 2. True, 3. False. General Fuzuki's eyes are actually stuck-on cake tins that the Moshling dozes behind, 4. True, 5. False. Rummaging Plotamuses are obsessed with digging up fluffles - precious toadstools that smell of liquorice, 6. False. Sooki-Yaki is a Caped Assassin.

Puzzle 86
THE M FACTOR
1.Tyra Fangs, 2. Mansion, 3. Underground Disco, 4. Judge, 5. Lowest Score, 6. Music

Puzzle 87
CAN HE NET IT? YES HE CAN!
41. Roxy has got caught in the Colonel's net.

Puzzle 88
PUZZLING POEM
Katsuma

Puzzle 89
WALDO'S WACKY WORD BOX

	1	2	3
1	Z	A	G
2	A	G	E
3	G	E	E

Puzzle 90
SEED SUDOKO

Puzzle 91
SNOOP SCOOP!
1. Tubby Huggishi Purdy eats her own body weight in pastry!
2. Like, wow! Cali hooks up Kissy and Flumpy. It's a moshmance made in heaven!
3. Squidge bites third Moshling victim this month!

Puzzle 92
NIFTY SHIFTY
MONSTROCITY

Puzzle 93
JEEPERS CREEPERS

Puzzle 94
CRAZY QUILT
A

Puzzle 95
SHAPE SHAKE
1. 18, 2. ■ , 3. ☆, 4. 8.

Puzzle 96
MOSHLING MEDITATIONS
1. A towel, 2. A kangaroo, 3. A cold, 4. Fire.

Puzzle 97
ANACROSSAGRAM

¹E	²O	³S	⁴N
²F	R	U	O
³S	T	O	R
⁴A	E	P	T

Puzzle 98
FLUFFY STUFF
1. B, 2. A, 3. B, 4. A, 5. C, 6. A, 7. C, 8. C.

Puzzle 99
JURASSIC LARKS

F	F	G	J	W	H	B	T	A	D	B
L	K	L	F	Z	R	G	P	K	V	J
A	Q	V	U	V	H	T	O	O	T	M
P	D	G	P	F	S	D	O	R	I	S
P	X	D	R	F	F	J	K	P	T	U
A	C	M	E	N	D	L	Y	H	R	R
S	K	E	H	K	G	R	E	F	S	U
A	A	C	I	U	M	M	S	F	L	A
U	E	I	S	M	U	K	O	O	N	S
R	U	M	T	V	D	N	N	S	L	Y
U	Q	E	O	M	E	C	M	S	X	K
S	S	T	R	J	E	G	S	I	J	N
D	P	A	I	Y	T	U	Y	L	K	I
R	I	L	C	I	M	R	G	F	G	H
S	P	O	G	A	U	G	D	H	U	T
X	T	C	T	T	T	L	V	C	K	A
J	L	O	Y	T	N	E	T	H	N	Y
P	L	H	G	Z	W	B	G	S	U	O
P	V	C	A	S	T	E	R	O	I	D

Puzzle 100
EYES SPY
54

Puzzle 101
LINE DANCE
12

Puzzle 102
A WEEK OF WILD WORDS
1. F, 2. G, 3. A, 4. D, 5. C, 6. E, 7. B

Puzzle 103
RHYME TIME
A Furi

Puzzle 104
SHUFFLE KERFUFFLE
GOOGENHEIM

Puzzle 105
PAPPED!

Puzzle 106
MOE'S MINUTE MAKEOVER
418 Rox

Puzzle 107
JIGSAW JAM
E

Puzzle 108
WALK THE PLANK
3 **(x3)** = 9 **(-4)** = 5 **(x4)** = 20 **(-4)** = 16 **(x5)** =
80 **(-4)** = 76 **(x6)** = 456 **(-4)** = 451

Puzzle 109
GROWL ON THE PROWL
1. Two, 2. A satellite dish, 3. Katsuma Krunch,
4. Triangular, 5. Three, 6. Upstairs in his mansion.

Puzzle 110
INTO THE GLOOP
1. GENERAL FUZUKI, 2. SHELBY
3. PEPPY, 4. CHERRY BOMB

Puzzle 111
WALDO'S WACKY WORD BOX

	1	2	3
1	E	W	E
2	W	A	G
3	E	G	G

Puzzle 112
ROX DROP
26

Puzzle 113
SKY SCRAMBLE

1. Angel
2. Squidge
3. Gurgle

Puzzle 114
THINKY PLINKY
B

Puzzle 115
CHOCK-A-BLOCK
186

Puzzle 116
SCARE SQUARES
32

Puzzle 117
KEN KEN AGAIN

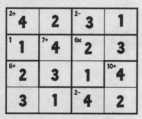

Puzzle 118
MANIC MATCH
5. None of the above. The correct sequence is:
AABCBAAADB
DAADDCBBCC
ACBBACDDAB
BBCCCADBBD

Puzzle 119
TRICKY TRIVIA
1. PRIDE, 2. VIENNA, 3. SEVEN, 4. CANADA

Puzzle 120
EYE EYE!
1. C, 2. E, 3. A, 4. B, 5. F, 6. D

Puzzle 121
POTTY PREDICTION
GO TO THE SEED CART AND BUY THREE RANDOM
SEEDS. PLANT THEM IN YOUR MOSHLING GARDEN
- YOU MIGHT BE LUCKY!

Puzzle 122
MAIN STREET MAYHEM
1. Pete Slurp and Lila Tweet, 2. Construction work
3. Colonel Catcher, 4. The newest Moshi
members, 5. A stall on the back of a bike,
6. Egon Groanay, 7. The Puzzle Palace.

Puzzle 123
CELEBRATION CROSSWORD

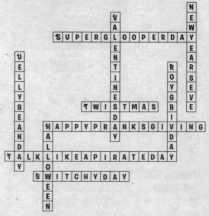

Puzzle 124
ALPHABET SOUP
1. U, 2. P, 3. G

Puzzle 125
SWEET SPOT

Puzzle 126
BLABBERING BIRDIES
1. Tiki, 2. Peppy, 3. DJ Quack, 4. Angel the Sky Pony. This heavenly creature might be gorgeous, but its certainly not a Birdie, 5. Prof. Purplex.

Puzzle 127
ALL THE OOZE THAT'S FIT TO PRINT
1. Tosh and tittle-tattle, 2. Ooze that's news,
3. Ooze that's news, 4. Tosh and tittle-tattle
5. Ooze that's news, 6. Ooze that's news.

Puzzle 128
SIX SNEAKY SNAKES
C

Puzzle 130
BOOM BOOM, SHAKE THE ROOM!

		¹G	A	M	E	S			
²O	O	H	L	A	L	A	N	E	
		³R	O	X					
	⁴D	I	A	V	L	O			
⁵O	C	T	O						
		⁶F	L	U	T	T	E	R	B	Y
⁷S	N	O	O	K	U	M	S		
	⁸B	U	M	B	L	C	H	O	P	S
⁹L	O	V	E	B	E	R	R	I	E	S

Puzzle 131
MISSIONS MATCH-UP

Mission 1	Missing Moshling Egg	B
Mission 2	Voyage Under Potion Ocean	F
Mission 3	Strangeglove From Above	D
Mission 4	Candy Catastrophe	J
Mission 5	Pop Goes The Goo Goo	A
Mission 6	Super Moshiversity Challenge	G
Mission 7	20,000 Leagues Under The Fur	I
Mission 8	Spooktacular Spectacular	E
Mission 9	Snow Way Out	H
Mission 10	Super Weapon Showdown	C

Puzzle 132
WORD WARP
1. ASCEND, 2. MEADOW, 3. SERPENT,
4. SCARLET, 5. SUNSET

Puzzle 133
TYRA'S HIP TIP
HORRODS MYSTERY EGGS ARE THE
MUST-HAVE CRAZE THIS SEASON!

Puzzle 134
I CAN SEE A RAINBOW...

Puzzle 135
GIFT ISLAND
1. Three, 2. Bert, 3. A red welcome banner held by smiling Moshlings, 4. Yellow, 5. On top of a pile of presents next to the Factory, 6. The Gift Island paddle steamer, 7. He is Gift Island's only scooter-based delivery monster, 8. Chick Checker the stork, 9. Green, 10. A wooden bridge.

Puzzle 136
CHA-CHING!
1. 237 Rox, 2. 28 Rox, 3. 5, 4. 150 minutes, 5. 20 Rox, 6. 11.25 centimetres

Puzzle 137
GETTING JIGGY WITH IT

Puzzle 138
BLOCK PARTY
E

Puzzle 139
WALL SCRAWL
BUY FLOOR POLISH FROM THE SNEEZE WAX
COMPANY AND SLICK IT ON!

Puzzle 140
COUNT YOUR PENNIES
15

Puzzle 141
BUSTER'S ALBUM
1. E, 2. C, 3. F, 4. A, 5. B, 6. D

Puzzle 142
POTTY FLOWERS IN A ROW
1. SNOOKUMS, 2. CUTIE PIE, 3. STANLEY,
4. SHISHI, 5. POOKY, 6. HUMPHREY,
7. LIBERTY, 8. HANSEL

Puzzle 143
MIXED-UP MOSHLINGS

1. Purdy
2. Fifi
3. Doris

Puzzle 144
BANGERS AND MASH
D

Puzzle 145
CRAZY QUILT
D

Puzzle 146
PULL-OUT PETS
Puppies: C, A, D, B
Kitties: E, D, B, A

Puzzle 147
GIUSEPPE GETAWAY

Puzzle 148
WALDO'S WACKY WORD BOX

	1	2	3
1	T	A	D
2	A	I	R
3	D	R	Y

Puzzle 149
LINE DANCE
16

Puzzle 150
FUNNY FACEWORD

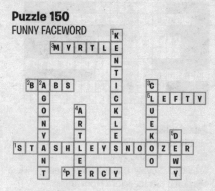

Puzzle 151
SHUFFLE KERFUFFLE
BEAU SQUIDDLY

Puzzle 152
BIG BAD BILL
1. A river, 2. The letter 'n'.

Puzzle 153
D IS FOR DRESS UP ROOM!

Glove mitts

Flamin' shades

Build-a-human ears

Welding mask

Puzzle 154
HERE BE MONSTERS

1. Moshi Fun Park, 2. The Port, 3. Ooh La Lane, 4. Gift Island, 5. The Volcano (Super Moshi HQ), 6. Sludge Street, 7. Main Street, 8. Candy Cane Caves

Puzzle 155
TRICKY TEXTS

1. 5 fingers on a hand, 2. 52 cards in a deck, 3. 8 planets in the Solar System, 4. 366 days in a Leap Year, 5. 11 players in a football team, 6. 26 letters in the alphabet

Puzzle 156
PERVERSE VERSE

Zommer

Puzzle 157
SHAPE SHAKE

A. Circle, B. 5, C. Hexagon, D. 7

Puzzle 158
MYSTERY MONSTER

Poppet

Puzzle 159
COUNT WITH CLUTCH

14

Puzzle 160
ANACROSSAGRAM

¹O	O	³D	⁴M
²O	G	L	N
³L	N	E	O
⁴P	G	N	O

Puzzle 161
CLEVERER THAN CLEO

1. A coffin
2. Breath
3. The letter 'm'
4. A human - as babies we crawl along on all fours, then we walk upright, before finally in old age using a walking stick!

Puzzle 162
TECHIE TEST

1. A, 2. C, 3. A, 4. A, 5. C, 6. B, 7. B, 8. B, 9. A, 10. B,

Puzzle 163
WOMBAT WORD SEARCH

WARRIOR Wombats are a mysterious type of **MOSHLING** that were once used to guard **ROX** and other precious things. General **FUZUKI** and his ilk are said to not need any **SLEEP** at night. Their eyes always seem open, but **BUSTER** Bumblechops' research has proved this is a sham! He has proved that their vigilant peepers are actually little **CAKE** tins welded on to their hats. If you want to attract one of these sleepyheads you'll have to work hard. Red Hot **SILLY** Peppers, **LOVE** Berries and Star **BLOSSOM** might tempt the Moshling into your garden.

```
F U Z U K I A R K J L W
D I F A M A G H B T V L
Q Z B L O S S O M M K O
G G R F G E T Y B Q P V
J M T W R Z G B U F Z E
F C Y B Z O N D S M K S
F A X L C D I S T I X D
T K C B L Y L R E O B G
D E D L R I H T R P R H
I D P E E L S C Q A T H
H B J T F G O V M E W Y
C S H W Y V M D X A O O
```

Puzzle 164
FLAG FRENZY

1. SWEDEN: Blue, Yellow
2. JAMAICA: Black, Yellow, Green
3. FRANCE: Red, White, Blue
4. CHINA: Red, Yellow

Puzzle 165
MATHS MASH

a. 78 + 12 = 936, b. 85 - **63** = 22,
c. 26 x 8 = **208**, d. 355 ÷ **5** = 71,
e. 739 + 478 = 1217, f. 1452 + **789** = 2241,
g. 188 ÷ 5 = 37.6, h. **33** x 58 = 1914

Puzzle 166
SHAPE SHAKE

1. ●, 2. 2, 3. Pentagon, 4. 12.

Puzzle 167
SECRET SUDUKO

Puzzle 168
STRANDED!
1. GAIL, 2. LENNY LARD, 3. TIDDLES,
4. BILLY BOB BAITMAN, 5. MR MEOWFORD

Puzzle 169
TRICKY TRIVIA
1. KING GEORGE IV, 2. EDINBURGH, 3. MAY
4. ASIA, 5. 11

Puzzle 170
EYES SPY
50

Puzzle 171
DEAR DIARY
Dear Diary,
What an awesome day - I lurrrrve writing for **SHRILLBOARD** Magazine! When I got to my desk, one of my most trusted Fluffy sources, **HONEY**, called to say that teen sensation **ZACK** Binspin had been spotted sipping bug juice in Ooh LA Lane!

Naturally I skedaddled right over there with Holga the **HAPPY** Snappy, primed and ready to shoot! The minute we arrived, the day just got even better! First Mr Binspin posed for some top pix, then he introduced us to his celebrity friend **AVRIL** LeScream from the **FIZZBANGS**! OMM!!!!! The two stars were totally divine - in fact, the three of us got on like a house on fire. Just as we were swapping digits, the rest of the band cruised by. Result? Three tickets to see them play at the Underground **DISCO**.

The band totally rocked, as did we! At the end, me and the stars made a date to meet at the same time next week. Yowzers!!!

Ruby Scribblez

Puzzle 172
BUBBLE TROUBLE
1. Ten, 2. FALSE, there are 46 white and 16 black. 3. 180, 4.

Puzzle 173
SQUISE SQUISH

Puzzle 174
ANAGROGRAM

¹S	H	²A	S
²H	A	³L	S
³O	M	N	E
⁴G	R	O	E

Puzzle 175
NIFTY SHIFTY
HE ONCE TOPPED THE TALLEST TOTEM POLE IN TIKKIHAAHAA

Puzzle 176
MONSTAR
MIRROR

Puzzle 177
BATTY BOXES
1. Up for grabs, 2. Once in a while
3. Great things come in small packages,
4. Toronto, 5. Broken Dreams, 6. Backwards

Puzzle 178
WHIRLY WORLDIES

Mini Ben is missing.

Puzzle 179
WHO AM I?
I'm Shelly Splurt

Puzzle 180
TRICKY TRIVIA
1. DA VINCI, 2. ASLAN, 3. BEETHOVEN
4. JACQUELINE WILSON, 5. DR FAUSTUS
(IT WAS WRITTEN BY CHRISTOPHER MARLOWE)

Puzzle 181
DEAR AGONY ANT
LETTER A is from Giuseppe Gelato
LETTER B is from Cali
LETTER C is from Tyra Fangs

Puzzle 182
BINSPIN DOODLES

Puzzle 183
EYES SPY
58

Puzzle 184
SACK THE STYLIST

Puzzle 185
MASTER OF MOSHI
A Tentacle Chair

Puzzle 186
BILLY BOB'S BOOTS
59

Puzzle 187
MOSHI MARATHON
1. DIAVLO, 2. POPPET, 3. KATSUMA,
4. LUVLI, 5. ZOMMER
Since Katsuma was third and Poppet came
second, Luvli could only have come first or
fourth. Since Luvli was behind Poppet, Luvli could
not have won, therefore she must have been
fourth. Zommer could not be first, second, third
or fourth so must have been fifth. If Zommer
was fifth, Luvli fourth, Katsuma third and Poppet
second then Diavlo must have won the race.
Furi must be the only Moshi that couldn't be
bothered to enter.

Puzzle 188
SUPER-FURRY ANIMAL
 It's the Shrewman

Puzzle 189
WALDO'S WACKY WORD BOX

	1	2	3
1	O	W	N
2	W	E	E
3	N	E	T

Puzzle 190
ANACROSSAGRAM

¹E	²N	³I	⁴R
²D	D	E	E
³D	E	R	E
⁴A	U	D	L

Puzzle 191
THE GENERAL'S GRID

A	B	C	D	E	F	G	H	I	J	K	L	M
HxW	Q÷T	>Y	T-L		I+J	F/N	E+N	K+T		H-E	Q+E
15	9	26	11	2	18	24	3	8	16	4	1	23

N	O	P	Q	R	S-	T	U	V	W	X	Y	Z
	>Q	E÷U	C-W	ExS	L+N	F-N	L+J		<N		G+L	>D
6	22	19	21	14	7	12	17	10	5	20	25	13

Puzzle 192
THE CURSE OF IGGY
50

Puzzle 193
SIMON SAYS
Max scored 7, Clem scored 4, Zach scored 9 and is the winner!

Puzzle 194
CHOCK-A-BLOCK
130

Puzzle 195
ELUSIVE EGG HEAD

It's Pooky the Playful Potty Pipsqueak.

Puzzle 196
D

Puzzle 197
LOOPY LINE-UP

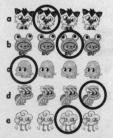

Puzzle 198
GROSS OUT WORDSEARCH

A	S	L	U	D	G	E	F	U	D	G	E
B	L	I	W	D	U	F	U	F	E	S	G
I	U	P	B	R	L	B	F	F	R	O	G
L	G	G	A	D	O	S	D	A	O	T	P
I	G	Y	J	O	L	I	E	T	A	S	L
H	O	N	A	U	L	B	T	D	S	A	A
C	E	Y	E	P	I	E	Y	E	T	O	N
Y	O	Y	L	M	P	C	M	E	B	R	T
L	O	O	M	R	L	P	E	N	E	W	K
L	S	U	Y	V	O	S	Y	P	A	L	O
I	C	R	X	H	P	F	D	O	S	H	O
S	L	O	P	N	I	T	A	W	T	S	H

Puzzle 199
PRINT PANIC
1. Furi's body, Katsuma's tail and Luvli's antennae. 2. Poppet's head, Diavlo's horns, Zommer's body. 3. Zommer's head, Luvli's wings, Poppet's body.

Puzzle 200
VOWEL HOWEL
SITE

Puzzle 201
THE STUFF OF LEGENDS
It's Tiddles! He started as bait on a fisherman's hook, but escaped to the bottom of the lake where he fed on algae – growing to 1,500 times his normal size. He now entertains the locals with his amazing yodelled songs.

Puzzle 202
CLOUD JUMPING

12 - 3 =   15 x 6 =   88 ÷ 4 =   87 ÷ 2 x 7 - 2.5 =   22 x 16 ÷ 2 =

Puzzle 203
LINE DANCE
12

Puzzle 204
BEACH PARTAY!

Puzzle 205
EYES SPY
59

Puzzle 206
GINGER WHINGER
FEED ME CHEESE OR FEEL MY WRATH

Puzzle 207
ELMORE'S CONUNDRUM
TEAM B: STOMPER AND CHOMPER

Puzzle 208
WHY SO GLUMP?

BRUISER · MUSTACHIO · NED · SQUIFF · PIRATE PONG · FISHLIPS

Puzzle 209
SPOT THE SCRAWLY DIFFERENCE

Puzzle 210
SCARE SQUARES
67

Puzzle 211
JEEPERS CREEPERS
There are 5 sets of Jeeper's eyes.
The hidden beastie is ShiShi.

Puzzle 212
HORRODS SHOPPING SPLURGE

Shakesfear's Bust	351 Rox
The Lava Lamp	55 Rox
Scream Shake Painting	153 Rox
Treasure Chest	103 Rox
Catacactus	117 Rox
Goggle Eyed Wall Trout	97 Rox
Totem Troll Urn	75 Rox

Puzzle 213
STOP PRESS

1. Moshi MonStars Announce World Tour. Zach Binspin to support.

2. Moshi MonStars to kick off tour with intimate gig at Underground Disco - guest list only

3. VAN SLAP VS DEMONSTA IN BIG BAND BUST-UP

Rockers the Moshi MonStars were involved in a mighty music mishap when Axl Van Slap accidentally dropped DJ Demonsta's decks when unloading the tour bus before their gig at the legendary Firebowl last night. The Katsuma refused to take the blame for dropping them, suggesting that Demonsta's mucky ways meant they were dripping in Toad Soda and slipped from his grasp!

Puzzle 214
WHOSE HOBBY IS IT ANYWAY?
Bubba - Practicing moves on his Dance, Dance Roarvolution machine.
Dizzy Bolt - Knitting and weightlifting
Art Lee - Chomping Spider Lollies in one bite
Dewy - Sipping Slug Slurp Slushies and reading back issues of *Hammer Times*
Clem - Listening to Hop-Hop music and working on robotic donut rigs

Puzzle 215
MIXED-UP MOSHLINGS

Cherry Bomb - aka The Baby Boomer, is a Noisie. These clockwork Moshlings fizz and crackle when excited. They're often found in Kaboom Canyon.

Nipper - is an ultra-rare Techie. Their stretchy arms make them versatile and helpful. They can also pluck Rox from the highest trees.

Tiamo - is a Smilie. She helps monsters in distress with her sparkling energy aura. Tiamo likes five pieces of fruit a day, but she thinks egg yolks are yucky.

Puzzle 216
MYRTLE TREASURE DIVING
1. Raarghly's spaceship
2. Billy Bob Baitman's old boot
3. Weevil Kneevil's bike
4. Fumble
5. Lenny Lard's rubber ring
6. Lefty's telescope

Puzzle 217
SECRET WORD
KIT

Puzzle 218
MOSHLING-TASTIC
48

Puzzle 219
IF YOUR NAME'S NOT DOWN, YOU AIN'T COMIN' IN!
1. A scar, 2. True, 3. Mom, 4. A spider web, 5. False. He has an anchor on his right forearm, 6. False, he has two upward pointing fangs.

Puzzle 220
LINE DANCE
21

Puzzle 221
FIND THE FLUFFLE
D

Puzzle 222
NINJA QUIZ
1.b, 2.a, 3.a, 4.c, 5.c, 6.b, 7.c, 8.a, 9.a, 10.b

Puzzle 223
FLAG FRENZY
1. Blue globe in a yellow shape on a green background
2. Yellow star on red
3. Red, white and blue union jack on a blue background with white stars
4. Green, white and red stripes

Puzzle 224
FOODIE LETTER LINK

		W	H	A	C	K	C	U	R	R	A	N	T	
				F	R	O	Z	E	N	D	E	S	S	E	R	T
				J	O	L	L	Y					
		S	P	A	R	K	L	E	P	O	P			
L	O	V	E	B	E	R	R	I	E	S				
				H	O	T							

Puzzle 225
CRASH, BANG, WALLOP!
46

Puzzle 226
SAFETY FIRST

Puzzle 227
A DAY TO REMEMBER
1. Twistmas, 2. National Jelly Bean Day, 3. It's on 9th April. Roy G. Biv rides into town to ensure Monstro City has rainbows for the rest of the year. 4. Switchy Day, 5. It commemorates the time when Elmore the Great fell and blocked the road into Monstro City. The Grub Lorry couldn't deliver food - until the Moshis Monsters and Moshlings worked together to pull him out of the way. They then feasted 'til sundown. 6. The Pilgrim's Hat

Puzzle 228
SAND SHAPES
1. Squidge - Furry Heebee - Spookies
2. Gurgle - Performing Flappasaurus - Dinos
3. Gabby - Mini Moshifone - Techies
4. McNulty - Undercover YapYap - Puppies
5. Peppy - Stunt Penguin - Birdies
6. Scamp - Froggie Doggie - Puppies